Spelling Rules!

Janelle Ho and
Helen Pearson

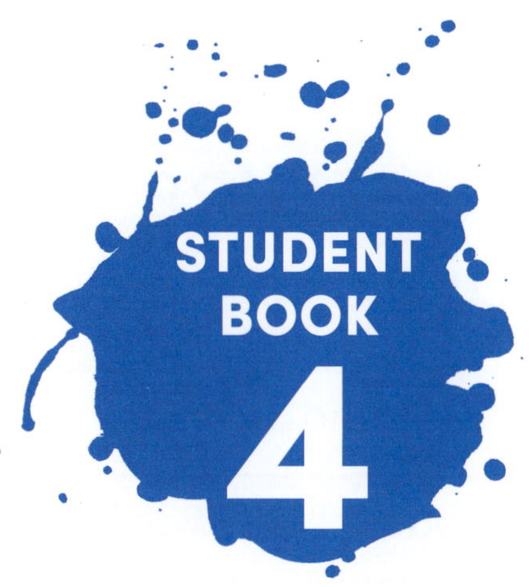

Australian Curriculum Edition

Name: ________________________________

Class: ________________________________

Contents

SLLURP

SLLURP summarises the spelling strategies that you can use to learn new words.

Say	Say the word carefully and slowly to yourself.
Listen	Listen to how each part of the word sounds in sequence.
Look	Look at the patterns of letters in the word and the shape of the word.
Understand	Understand rules, word meanings and word origins.
Remember	Remember all the similar words you can already spell and relate this knowledge to any new word.
Practise	Practise writing the word until it is firmly fixed in your long-term memory.

Scope and Sequence

Unit	Skill Focus: Vowels	Consonants	Letter patterns	Morphology and etymology	Homophones/ Confusing words	Topic words	WORD LIST
1	two-syllable words with long sounds, silent e			-s, -es, -ed, -ing: dropping silent e			oppose, endure, revise, complete, arrange, escape, persuade, realise, collide, assume, include, declare
2	short and long y		ay, ey, oy	-s, -es, -ed, -ing: changing y to i	pray/prey		copy, hurry, guilty, mystery, variety, deny, apply, simplify, qualify, display, prey, annoy
3				adding -ed, -ing to two-syllable words: doubling final consonant			begin, forget, regret, occur, prefer, enter, offer, visit, happen, target, label, detail
4		words ending in lf	ph, gh	phobia			engulf, behalf, cough, trough, phase, phobia, phantom, metaphor, emphasise, biography, amphibian, sophisticated
5		words ending in double consonants		-er, -est			odd, stiff, err, recall, install, swell, thrill, floss, discuss, possess, witness, embarrass
6	REVISION						
7	ea			led/lead, weather/ whether			least, eager, release, dread, ahead, heavy, health, meant, instead, pleasant, jealous, weather
8				-ion, -ness; *claudere*			direction, suggestion, location, separation, confusion, decision, conclusion, greatness, selfishnesss, stubbornness, cleanliness, forgetfulness
9		j	ge, dge, dj				bandage, sponge, surge, stranger, siege, badger, pledge, reject, injection, adjust, conjunction, adjective
10				un-, in-, dis-; *videre*			unfamiliar, undeveloped, unbroken, unquestioning, inactive, incomplete, informal, invisible, disease, disqualify, discontented, discontinue
11					confusing pairs		lose, loose, breath, breathe, desert, dessert, practise, practice, wonder, wander, stationery, stationary
12	REVISION						
13	oa, ou		ow		fowl/foul		narrow, sorrow, tomorrow, loan, poach, coward, foul, announce, voucher, boundary, council, knowledge
14			er/ear				verse, superb, alert, convert, deserve, determined, certain, permanent, earthquake, research, earnest, rehearsal
15			or, ur, our	court-			worthy, senior, surprise, further, burden, survive, journal, flavour, labour, courtesy, honour, nourish
16			words ending in ure	thermo-, -meter			nature, future, capture, failure, creature, feature, measure, pleasure, leisure, adventure, furniture, temperature
17						colours, similes	ruby, scarlet, lilac, violet, emerald, indigo, crimson, azure, khaki, ochre, turquoise, sapphire
18	REVISION						
19				-th	fourth/forth	ordinal numbers	fourth, fifth, eighth, ninth, twelfth, growth, warmth, length, strength, width, depth, breadth
20			words ending in ic	-ic; -ed, -ing: adding k			panic, picnic, magic, logic, critic, basic, mimic, fantastic, terrific, energetic, automatic, enthusiastic
21			words ending in al	-al, il-, un-			capital, hospital, final, logical, magical, national, natural, digital, criminal, critical, survival, emotional
22				-th, hyphenation		numbers	eleven, twelve, thirteen, fourteen, fifteen, twenty, thirty, forty, fifty, ninety, hundred, thousand
23		double consonants			accept/except, affect/effect		accept, accuse, attempt, attitude, pollute, approach, disappoint, opportunity, necessary, recommend, occasion, aggressive
24	REVISION						
25		soft g	words ending in ous				ginger, gently, general, average, generous, religion, intelligent, fragile, generation, advantage, emergency, gymnasium
26				-ous; rules for adding -ous			serious, precious, delicious, famous, nervous, dangerous, courageous, furious, cautious, envious, spacious, various
27				-en, -ise: rules for adding -en, ise; *memor*			lessen, stiffen, toughen, sadden, awaken, straighten, finalise, memorise, fantasise, energise, sympathise, visualise
28				-ment			movement, statement, argument, amazement, measurement, government, environment, treatment, development, attachment, encouragement, disappointment
29				compound words; abbreviations		computers	computer, laptop, email, internet, mobile, keyboard, program, download, insert, delete, icon, archive
30	REVISION						
31	ie, ei			rain/rein/reign			niece, belief, achieve, alien, receipt, deceive, protein, weird, reign, seize, beige, feisty
32			ex				exist, exchange, examination, explosion, expensive, exaggerate, excursion, exceed, except, extinct, exhausted, exhibition
33				-or, -er, -ant, -ian, -ist; apostrophes		occupations; non-English words	author, grocer, carpenter, lawyer, assistant, accountant, electrician, politician, journalist, pharmacist, chef, pilot
34						holidays	travel, relax, journey, caravan, luggage, budget, museum, attraction, entertainment, accommodation, sightseeing, restaurant
35	REVISION						

Note to Teachers and Parents

Spelling Rules!

Some students are natural spellers. But the vast majority of students need formal, systematic and sequential instruction about the way spelling works and the strategies they can use to become independent, confident spellers and spelling risk-takers.

The *Spelling Rules!* program is based on sound linguistic and pedagogical theory. It is informed by research into how students of different ages acquire and apply spelling skills, and how those skills move from the working to the long-term memory. The program closely follows the Australian English curriculum. *Australian Curriculum: English* references are provided in the Teacher Resource Books. The program consists of seven student books, fully supported by two Teacher Resource Books.

Each student book contains units of work, with each unit designed to be used over the course of a week. The content of each unit simultaneously develops new skills and reinforces skills from previous units. The introduction of new sounds and letter patterns is logically sequenced and takes into account both frequency of use and complexity. Where appropriate, topic words from other curriculum areas such as mathematics, science and social sciences are included. When spelling rules are introduced, only known sounds and letter patterns are used so that students focus on one skill at a time. Regular revision units enable teachers to assess student progress and reinforce key rules and patterns from previous units.

The *Spelling Rules!* program also incorporates elements of self-assessment. A simple reflection activity allows students to assess their own progress and provides you with a starting point for discussion.

Spelling knowledge

Learning to spell involves developing different kinds of spelling knowledge:

- **Kinaesthetic knowledge** – the physical feeling when saying different sounds and words, and when writing the shapes of letters and words
- **Phonological knowledge** – how a word sounds and the patterns of sounds in words
- **Visual knowledge** – how letters and words look and the visual patterns in words
- **Morphemic knowledge** – the meaning or function of words or parts of words
- **Etymological knowledge** – the origins and history of words and the effect this has on spelling patterns.

Icons used in Student Book 4

The following icons identify the main spelling strategy that students will use to complete an activity.

Say the word. (Kinaesthetic knowledge) These activities ask students to experience how sounds feel in the mouth and jaw. Changing the positions of the jaw, lips and tongue changes the sounds we make. Encourage students to pronounce the sounds and words accurately. If they mispronounce a sound or word, they may misrepresent it in writing.

Listen to the word. (Phonological knowledge) These activities focus on discriminating between different sounds and breaking up words into syllables or individual sound segments (phonemes).

Look at the word. (Visual knowledge) These activities help students to see how the sound is represented using combinations of letters, and to associate this visual pattern with what they are hearing. Students will develop the ability to know when a word does or does not 'look right'.

Understand the word. (Morphemic and etymological knowledge) These activities focus on word meanings, word families, prefixes and suffixes, spelling rules, word origins and so on, which help embed spelling in the long-term memory.

Practise writing the word. (Kinaesthetic knowledge) These activities develop students' awareness of the physical movement involved in writing the word. By practising writing the word a number of times and in different contexts, the spelling becomes embedded in the long-term memory.

This icon highlights useful spelling rules.

This icon tells students that a special clue or hint is provided for an activity. It may be a spelling, grammar or punctuation convention, or a definition of a useful term.

Encourages students to assess their progress across each unit.

Spelling Rules! Student Book 4 (ISBN 9780655092704) © Janelle Ho, Helen Pearson

Student Book 4

Units of work

Student Book 4 contains 35 weekly units of work. See the **Scope and Sequence chart** on page 3 for more information. Each revision unit gives students an opportunity to self-assess.

Word lists

In *Student Book 4*, each unit (except Revision) has a list of spelling words. The core words in the lists have been chosen to support the learning focus and strategies being taught in the unit.

Spelling lists enable a spelling element to be focused on, and provide sufficient examples to consolidate the teaching point. Topic words come from other curriculum areas, such as mathematics and social sciences. In addition, homophones and words that are easily confused with each other are explained and practised.

SLLURP

Each word list begins with a reminder for students to SLLURP. SLLURP summarises the strategies that will help spelling move from students' working memory to their long-term memory. These strategies are provided on page 2, for easy reference.

Unit at a glance

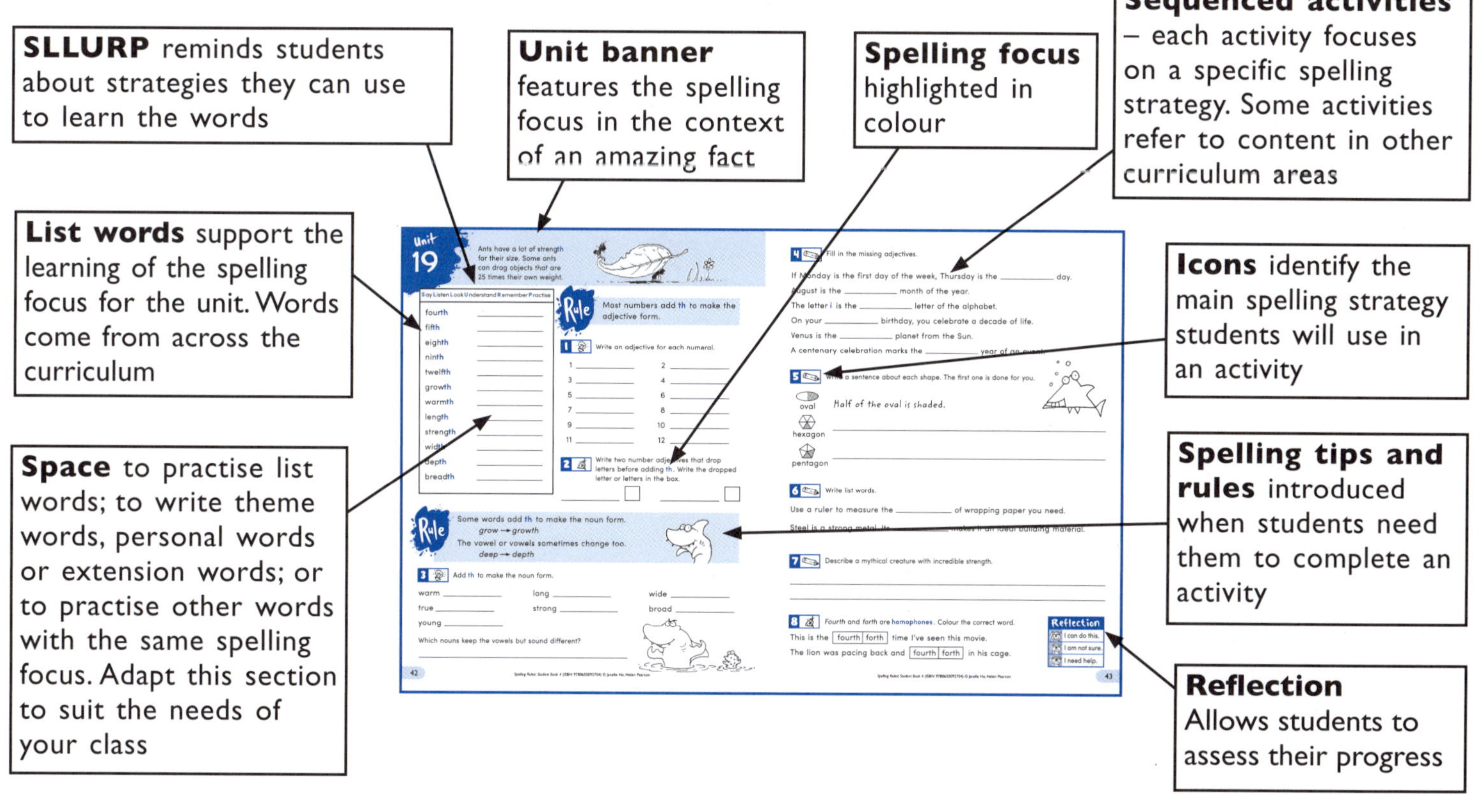

Spelling Rules! Teacher Resource Book 3–6

Full teacher support for *Student Book 4* is provided by *Spelling Rules! Teacher Resource Book 3–6*. Here you will find valuable background information about spelling development and spelling knowledge, along with practical resources, such as:

- teaching tips for every unit in *Student Book 4*
- extra word lists
- strategies for teaching spelling
- guidelines for assessment and diagnosis of errors
- activities to support struggling spellers
- worthwhile extension for more able spellers.

Unit 1

In China in 3000 BCE, children had powdered smallpox scabs stuck up their noses to make them immune to the horrible disease smallpox. It worked!

Say **L**isten **L**ook **U**nderstand **R**emember **P**ractise

oppose	______
endure	______
revise	______
complete	______
arrange	______
escape	______
persuade	______
realise	______
collide	______
assume	______
include	______
declare	______

1 Group list words using the final vowel sound.

a as in day
______
______
______

i as in by
______
______
______

e as in bead
______

o as in soap
______

u as in dew
______
______

list words left over
______
______

2 Write a list word that rhymes.

flows	strange	maid	replied	repair
______	______	______	______	______

3 Divide these list words into syllables. Underline the stressed syllable. For double consonants in the middle of a word, the syllable break comes between the double letters. *as/sume*

realise	suppose	declare	revise
arrange	conclude	collide	escape

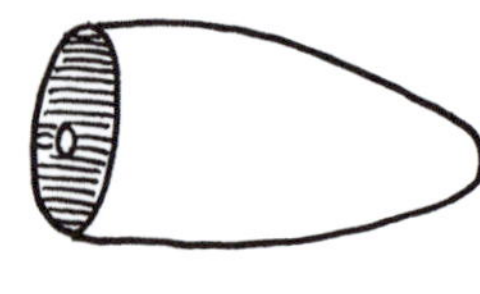
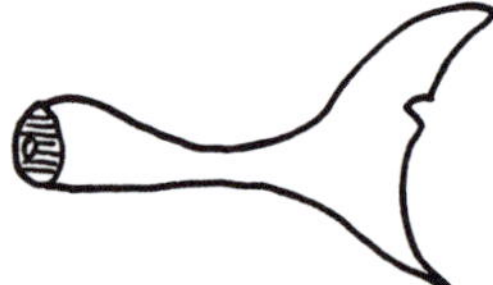

Spelling Rules! Student Book 4 (ISBN 9780655092704) © Janelle Ho, Helen Pearson

4 Antonyms are words with opposite meanings. Make antonyms by adding missing letters.

in _ _ ude → e _ cl _ d _ ins _ _ t → del _ t _

inc _ ea _ e → d _ cr _ _ s _ s _ p _ _ ate → c _ mb _ n _

If a word ends in silent **e**, drop the **e** before adding the suffixes **ed** or **ing**.

5 Complete the table.

word	add ed	add ing
waste	wasted	wasting
oppose		
realise		
endure		
complete		
arrange		
collide		

6 Add **s**, **ed** or **ing** to the word in brackets.

No one ________________ the student dressed as a clown. (recognise)

'Stop ________________ me whenever you lose something!' Vicki yelled. (blame)

Each class is ________________ to perform an item at assembly. (require)

When a chess piece is captured, it is ________________ from the board. (remove)

7 Add vowels to make words that match the clues.

r _ sc _ _ save from danger

pr _ v _ d _ supply

r _ t _ t _ turn

p _ rf _ m _ pleasant fragrance

r _ m _ v _ take away

_ ll _ str _ t _ draw

Unit 2

Nobody knows for certain how the pyramids in Egypt were built. It remains a mystery!

Say Listen Look Understand Remember Practise	
copy	
hurry	
guilty	
mystery	
variety	
deny	
apply	
simplify	
qualify	
display	
prey	
annoy	

Rule If the word has a single vowel followed by a single consonant, double the consonant before adding **y**. *mud → muddy*

1 Make adjectives by adding **y**. Remember to follow the rule you have just learnt.

hair	shine	dirt
______	______	______
fur	risk	guilt
______	______	______
mess	spot	noise
______	______	______
itch	grub	droop
______	______	______

Rule If a word ends in **y**, change **y** to **i** before adding **es** or **ed**. Keep the **y** when adding **ing**.

2 Complete the table.

word	add es	add ed	add ing
hurry			
deny			
reply			
simplify			
qualify			

Spelling Rules! Student Book 4 (ISBN 9780655092704) © Janelle Ho, Helen Pearson

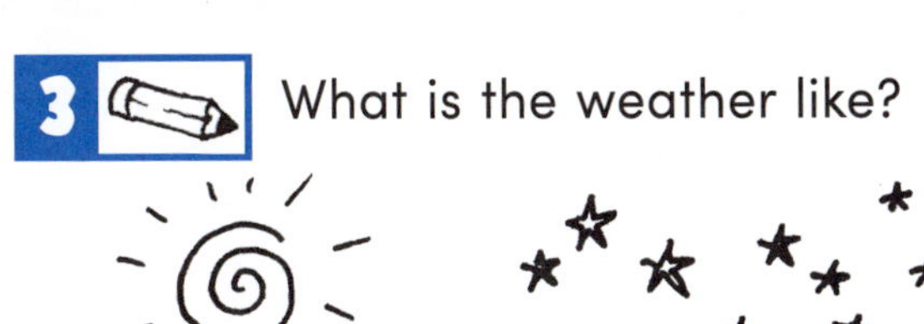

What is the weather like?

Rewrite each sentence, replacing the underlined word with a list word.

Troy felt regretful that his ball had broken his neighbour's window.

Grandma's patchwork quilts have a range of colours and patterns.

What happened to Sally's keys is a puzzle.

Of all the animals on show, my favourite is the giraffe.

Don't bother Amy while she is coding her robot.

Rewrite each sentence in the plural.

There is only one variety of apple in the store.

Auntie made a copy of the recipe for Mum.

I have a fantasy about what I want to be when I grow up.

prey and **pray** are homophones. Write the correct homophone.

As the king of the jungle, the lion has many ______________.

You can't just ______________. You also have to work hard!

The plural form of **prey** does not change. Such words are known as

____

Reflection

I can do this.

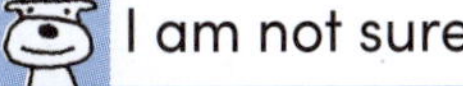
I am not sure.

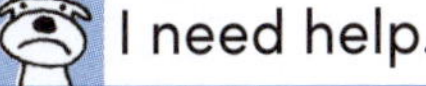
I need help.

Unit 3

The left side of your body is controlled by the right side of your brain.

Say Listen Look Understand Remember Practise	
begin	____________
forget	____________
regret	____________
occur	____________
prefer	____________
enter	____________
offer	____________
answer	____________
visit	____________
happen	____________
target	____________
label	____________
detail	____________

1 Each word has two syllables. Say each word and draw a line between the syllables. Underline the stressed syllable. *ga|llop*

begin regret occur

excel forget admit

When adding **ed** or **ing**, double the final consonant if:

1. the stress is on the final syllable and
2. the final syllable has one vowel.

occur → occurred, occurring

2 Complete the table.

add ed	add ing
travel ____________	expel ____________
permit ____________	regret ____________

3 Write three list words that have a short final vowel sound. Write three list words that have a long final vowel sound.

short final vowel	long final vowel
____________	____________
____________	____________
____________	____________

If the final syllable has two vowels, just add **ed** or **ing**.

appeal → appealed, appealing

4 Complete the table.

add ed	add ing
appear ____________	complain ____________
detail ____________	reveal ____________

Spelling Rules! Student Book 4 (ISBN 9780655092704) © Janelle Ho, Helen Pearson

5  Add a suffix to each list word. Use the rules to decide if the final consonant should be doubled. The stressed syllable is underlined.

word	add ed
prefer	
happen	
enter	
regret	
visit	
target	

word	add ing
begin	
forget	
offer	
occur	
label	
detail	

A word family consists of words that share the same base word.

act, actor, action, acting, acted, active, react

6 Complete each sentence using a word from the same word family as the word in brackets.

People sometimes get ______________ as they get older. (forget)

Mum is making a special dessert because we are having ______________. (visit)

Rani wanted to learn guitar so she joined a class for ______________. (begin)

Sean said he would meet me at the ______________ to the swimming pool. (enter)

You must wear ______________ goggles for this experiment. (safe)

7 Use list words to answer the questions.

Which word uses the same vowel sound twice? ______________

Which two words have the same meaning?

______________ and ______________

Reflection

I can do this.

I am not sure.

I need help.

The fear of amphibians is known as batrachophobia.

Say Listen Look Understand Remember Practise	
engulf	______
behalf	______
cough	______
trough	______
phase	______
phobia	______
phantom	______
metaphor	______
emphasise	______
biography	______
amphibian	______
sophisticated	______

1 Say each word aloud. Circle the word if you do not say the l.

calf wolf self
half gulf shelf

2 Write f, ff, gh or ph.

roo___ cli___ gra___
blu___ ___rase ___inish
dwar___ lau___ ___ield
rou___ brie___ ___oto

Which digraph cannot begin a word?

____

3 Use the rules to write the plural word.

loaf ______
self ______
calf ______
hoof ______
sniff ______
wharf ______

When a word ends in f, lf or fe, the f or fe usually changes to v before adding es to make the word plural.

leaf → leaves *elf → elves*
half → halves

When a word ends in ff, add s to make the word plural.

cliff → cliffs

Add s to make these words plural.

gulf → gulfs *proof → proofs*
chief → chiefs *belief → beliefs*
reef → reefs *roof → roofs*

4 Write the list words that are only nouns.

______ ______ ______ ______
______ ______ ______ ______

Spelling Rules! Student Book 4 (ISBN 9780655092704) © Janelle Ho, Helen Pearson

5 Use the clues to find **ph** words that complete the puzzle. Use a dictionary if you need help.

- a stage of development
- a group of words
- another word for ghost
- a wild bird you can eat
- a medical doctor
- a person who works in a pharmacy
- a person who studies philosophy

6 The word **phobia** is both a word and a word part. It can be combined with other word parts to describe different types of fear. Use a dictionary to write the meanings.

arachnophobia ______________________________

acrophobia ______________________________

nyctophobia ______________________________

ophidophobia ______________________________

7 Proofread this story. The text has five words that are incorrect. Circle the mistakes. Then write the correct spelling of the words in the boxes.

Mrs Berg's neffew tragically became an orfan when his parents died while swimming with dolfins. The dangers had been emfasised but their love of wildlife meant they took risks as fotografers. Ralph lives with the Bergs now.

8 Colour the correct word.

Our team scored a goal in each of the two | halfs | half's | halves | of the match.

I have so many books I need more | shelfs | shelf's | shelves |.

A | wolfs | wolf's | wolves | eyesight is better than a human's.

Cliff's | sniffs | sniff's | are loud and annoying.

Can we go fishing | of | off | the wharf on Saturday?

Reflection

- I can do this.
- I am not sure.
- I need help.

Unit 5

Levi Spear Parmly recommended using a waxen silk thread to floss. That was in 1819.

Say **L**isten **L**ook **U**nderstand **R**emember **P**ractise

odd	________
stiff	________
err	________
recall	________
install	________
swell	________
thrill	________
floss	________
discuss	________
possess	________
witness	________
embarrass	________

Tip A syllable that has double consonants at the end has a single vowel.

odd not *oodd* *swell* not *sweell*

1 Correct the following words.

stieff	flooss	stil
________	________	________
discuess	witnes	poesess
________	________	________

2 Unscramble the letters to make a word that ends in a double consonant.

lrhitl	slepl	slnailt
________	________	________
sarbs	fastf	darseds
________	________	________

Tip The suffixes **er** and **est** are added to words to compare two or more things.

kind kinder kindest

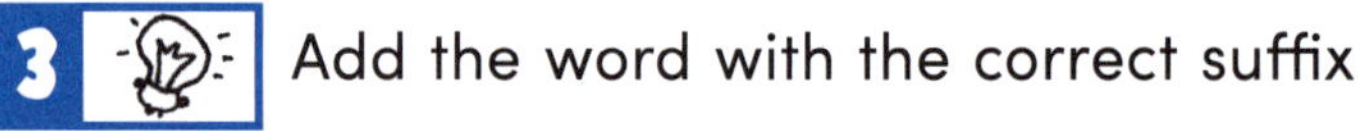

3 Add the word with the correct suffix.

It's odd to see Joe with short hair but it's ________ to see him wearing a shirt and tie!

There are many dull books on the shelf. Unfortunately for me, I think I picked the ________.

Tip Some words that end in double consonants need to add **y** first.

mess messy messier messiest

4 Write the correct form of the adjective.

Jess says Ben is the ________ player on the field. (boss)

Mr Cross is ________ than Mr Bell about how we present our work. (fuss)

Spelling Rules! Student Book 4 (ISBN 9780655092704) © Janelle Ho, Helen Pearson

5 An anagram is a word or phrase in which the letters can be rearranged to form another word or phrase. Write a list word for each anagram.

nil salt	its news	caller	bears arms
______	______	______	______

  Add the suffix.

	add **s** or **es**
chill	
add	
bluff	
witness	
discuss	

	add **ed**	add **ing**
swell		
install		
stuff		
stress		
embarrass		

7 Use the clues to write list words.

Which word has the antonym of short? ______

Which word has a donkey in it? ______

Which word has sickness in it? ______

Which word has the antonym of sickness? ______

 Imagine you have witnessed a robbery. Write your eyewitness account.

______

______

______

______

______

9 *re + call = recall*

Write other words that use the prefix **re**.

______

______

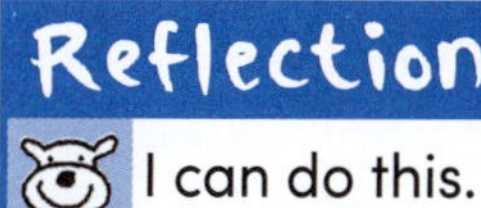

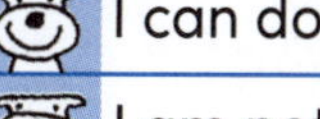 I can do this.

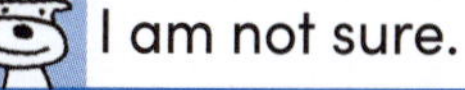 I am not sure.

 I need help.

Unit 6 Revision

Laughter is great exercise. It increases your heart rate, lowers your blood pressure and gives your face and stomach muscles a good workout!

1 An **f** sound can be written as **f**, **ff**, **gh** or **ph**. Write the correct letter or letters to complete each word.

sni___ whar___ ___rase rou___ meta___or

beha___ lau___ o___ten dwar___ autogra___

2 Sort the words into three groups.

target assume excite trophy disease surprise

verb only

______
______

verb or noun

______
______

noun only

______
______

3 Write the plural.

slide ______
graph ______
mystery ______
shelf ______
belief ______
witness ______

4 Write each verb so that it agrees with the new subject.

we annoy, she ______
I prefer, it ______
they forget, he ______
you recognise, she ______
I cough, he ______
you qualify, she ______

5 Write sentences. First use the word as a noun. Then use it as a verb.

laugh (noun) ______________________________

laugh (verb) ______________________________

visit (noun) ______________________________

visit (verb) ______________________________

6 Write an antonym.

exit ____________ admit ____________ exclude ____________

finish ____________ predator ____________ soften ____________

incomplete ____________ remember ____________ question ____________

7 Write the correct form of the word to complete each sentence.

Were you ____________ when you won the prize? (surprise)

I had a most ____________ holiday last summer. (excite)

We stopped when we saw Mr Tang ____________ down the corridor. (hurry)

When our neighbour's cat meows, Rover ____________ by barking. (reply)

The tennis final is ____________ right now. I am ____________ not bringing a hat to school because I am not ____________ to sit with my class to watch it. (happen, regret, allow)

8 Write about something you did that you feel guilty about.

____

____

____

____

Unit 7

The average person has about 100 000 dreams in their lifetime.

Say Listen Look Understand Remember Practise

least	______
eager	______
release	______
dread	______
ahead	______
heavy	______
health	______
meant	______
instead	______
pleasant	______
jealous	______
weather	______

1 Make words using the letters from each shape.

r l h thr spr tr

____ead ____ead ____ead

____ead ____ead ____ead

l lt f d th r

dea____ dea____ dea____

dea____ dea____ dea____

w sp st sn squ fr

____eak ____eak ____eak

____eak ____eak ____eak

2 Write the list words under the correct heading.

ea sound as in leaf

______

______

______

ea sound as in head

______ ______

______ ______

______ ______

______ ______

______

Spelling Rules! Student Book 4 (ISBN 9780655092704) © Janelle Ho, Helen Pearson

3 Make a new word. Circle the new word if the vowel sound has changed.

mean + t ______ seat + w ______ heal + th ______ breath + e ______ tread + h ______

4 Write a list word with the same meaning.

talk ______

keen ______

unable to hear ______

nice ______

5 Write a list word with the opposite meaning.

illness ______

most ______

light ______

behind ______

6 Write list words.

This New Year's Day we are going to a restaurant ______ of having a picnic.

Regular visits to the dentist are important for our dental ______.

7 *Weather* and *whether* are **homophones**. Write the correct word in each sentence.

Dean loves movies, ______ they are dramas or comedies.

I hope the ______ will be fine for our excursion.

Homographs are words with the same spelling but different meanings.

lead (sounds like bead) = go first, show someone the way

lead (sounds like head) = a heavy metal

In addition, the words *led* (past tense of lead) and *lead* (a metal) are **homophones**.

8 Write a sentence for both meanings of *lead* and for *led*.

______

______

______

______

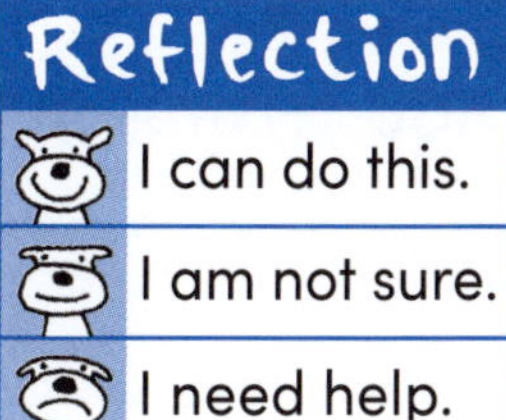

Unit 8

Before the compass was invented, explorers worked out the direct**ion**s using the sun during the day and the stars at night.

Say **L**isten **L**ook **U**nderstand **R**emember **P**ractise

direct**ion** ____________
suggest**ion** ____________
locat**ion** ____________
separat**ion** ____________
confus**ion** ____________
decis**ion** ____________
conclus**ion** ____________
great**ness** ____________
selfish**ness** ____________
stubborn**ness** ____________
cleanli**ness** ____________
forgetful**ness** ____________

Some verbs can be changed into nouns by adding **ion**.

act → action

If the verb ends in silent **e**, drop the **e** before adding **ion**.

create → creation

1  Complete the table.

verb	noun
complete	
direct	
	confusion
perfect	
	separation
	prevention
locate	
relate	

Rule

If the verb ends in **de**, change **de** to **s** before adding **ion**.

divide → division

2  Write the noun to complete each sentence.

In most sports, the referee's ____________ is final. (decide)

Olga wrote an exciting ____________ to her story. (conclude)

The ____________ of Sammi probably helped us win the Spelling Bee. (include)

There was a loud ____________, but luckily no one was hurt. (explode)

3 Each word has one or two suffixes. Circle each suffix.

carelessness

greatness thoughtlessness stubbornness forgetfulness

4 Add either **ion** or **ness** to make a noun. Use a dictionary if you need help.

awkward ______________ dizzy ______________ desperate ______________

discuss ______________ cheerful ______________ extend ______________

The word *conclude* means *to come to an end*. It comes from the Latin word *claudere,* which means *to close.*

5 Add the correct prefix. Use the definitions to help you.

_____clude: contain or add to _____clude: keep out or leave out

These words are opposite in meaning. They are ______________________________

Write a sentence using one of the words.

____

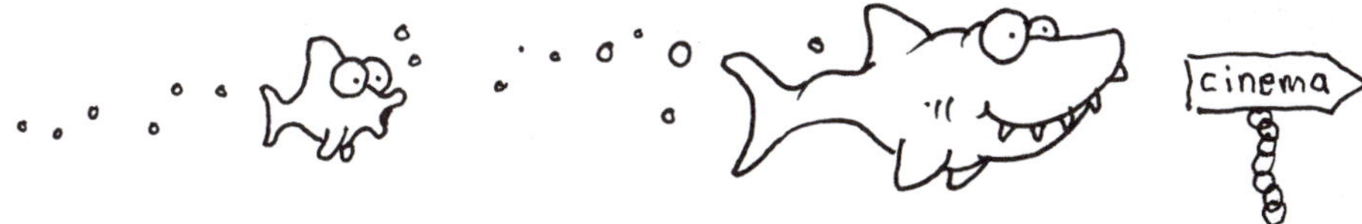

6 These sentences are too long. Rewrite them using a list word. The underlined words in the first two sentences are hints.

Can you tell me <u>in what street or building I would find</u> the cinema?

____

Writing our project was hard because Eng <u>refused to change his mind about some things</u>.

____

I often ask my family for their thoughts and ideas for my writing.

____

All cafés receive a rating based on how clean they are.

____

Unit 9

The Great Wall of China is so large it runs for more than 8000 kilometres!

Say **L**isten **L**ook **U**nderstand **R**emember **P**ractise

bandage	______
sponge	______
surge	______
stranger	______
siege	______
badger	______
pledge	______
reject	______
injection	______
adjust	______
conjunction	______
adjective	______

Rule

When **g** is followed by **e** or **i**, it usually makes a soft **g** sound.

page *magic* *giant*

But sometimes **g** before **e** or **i** makes a hard **g** sound.

gear *girl*

1 Group the words according to the sound **g** makes.

great angry ginger together
genius strange imagine agree

soft **g** ______ ______
______ ______

hard **g** ______ ______
______ ______

2 Write two words with the same vowel sound. Use a list word and a word of your own.

word	such	dirt	shame	wheel
list word				
my word				

Shark

Dark

3 Write list words.

Write the word that can be an adjective or a noun. ______

Write the words that are verbs only. ______ ______

Spelling Rules! Student Book 4 (ISBN 9780655092704) © Janelle Ho, Helen Pearson

4 Write the plural.

word	plural
bandage	
sponge	
siege	
stranger	
emergency	

5 Write the past tense.

word	past tense
surge	
pledge	
damage	
adjust	
budget	

6 Rearrange the letters to make a word. Each word has a soft **g** sound.

Angela pushed her __________ off her face so she could see the actors on
finger

the __________ more clearly. The hero was in great __________.
gates garden

Tip

A **conjunction** joins word, phrases or clauses. Here are some common conjunctions:

and nor but or so if because although

7 Write a conjunction to complete the sentence.

We are going to the local market to buy some meat __________ fruit. We want to walk there __________ it's raining, __________ Dad insists we have to drive. Luckily, the rain becomes lighter. Dad agrees we can walk __________ we each have a raincoat __________ an umbrella.

8 Circle the mistake in each sentence. Write the correct word.

Lucy redjected Jim's apology because she was still angry. __________

This year, every class will plege to raise $150. __________

Our family gets our flu ingections every year. __________

Use a soapy sponje to clean the stain. __________

Only a jenius can solve the mystery! __________

Reflection

- I can do this.
- I am not sure.
- I need help.

Unit 10

Diseases of the heart and blood vessels are the leading cause of death in the world.

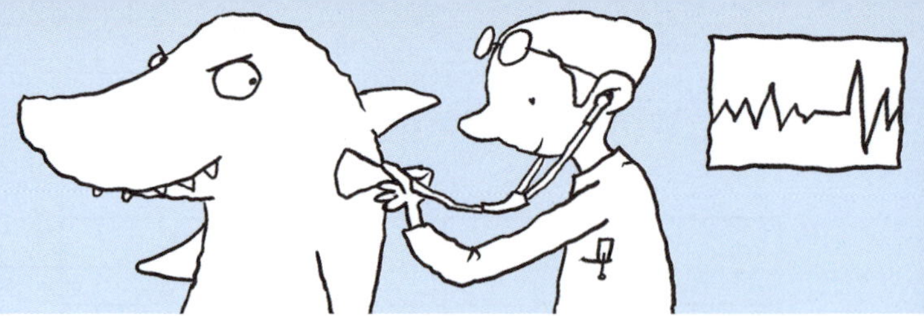

Say Listen Look Understand Remember Practise	
unfamiliar	______
undeveloped	______
unbroken	______
unquestioning	______
inactive	______
incomplete	______
informal	______
invisible	______
disease	______
disqualify	______
discontented	______
discontinue	______

Tip A prefix is placed in front of a word and changes its meaning. **un-**, **in-** and **dis-** are all prefixes.

1  Write the list words as prefix + base word. One has been done for you.

unfamiliar → un + familiar

undeveloped → ____ + ______

unbroken → ____ + ______

unquestioning → ____ + ______

inactive → ____ + ______

incomplete → ____ + ______

informal → ____ + ______

invisible → ____ + ______

disease → ____ + ______

disqualify → ____ + ______

discontented → ____ + ______

discontinue → ____ + ______

Tip A suffix is added to the end of a word. **-s**, **-ed**, **-ing**, **-er**, **-ion** and **-ness** are suffixes.

2  Break the words up into base word + suffix. Write another word by changing or adding a suffix.

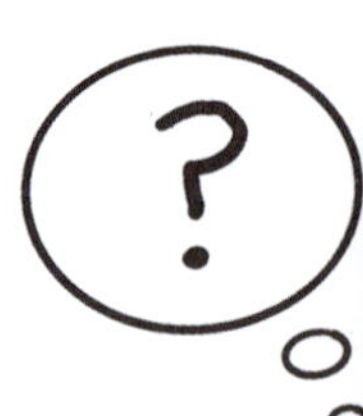

developed ______ + ____ ______

questioning ______ + ____ ______

contented ______ + ____ ______

active ______ + ____ ______

formal ______ + ____ ______

Spelling Rules! Student Book 4 (ISBN 9780655092704) © Janelle Ho, Helen Pearson

The word *visible* means *capable of being seen.* It comes from the Latin word *videre,* which means *to see.*

3 Use a word from the box to complete the sentences.

vision	visual	visible

Tina has 20/20 ______________, which means she can see perfectly.

Jupiter is sometimes ______________ on a clear night in the country.

I love walks that provide ______________ guides about which animals and plants to look out for.

4 These sentences are silly. Rewrite them using a list word. You may need to add a suffix.

The council wants to build a school in the green busy field.

____

Mum is annoyed because I've finished my homework.

____

Joey started running before the whistle, so he was awarded first prize.

____

Ellen couldn't sing the song without looking at the words because she knew it by heart.

____

Tom's party is a fancy dress party, so it will be serious.

____

Write **dis**, **in** or **un**.

_____easy

_____please

_____organised

_____likely

_____appoint

_____accurate

_____comfortable

_____dependent

Reflection

- I can do this.
- I am not sure.
- I need help.

Unit 11

Some turtles can **breathe** through their bottoms when underwater.

Say Listen Look Understand Remember Practise	
lose	________
loose	________
breath	________
breathe	________
desert	________
dessert	________
practise	________
practice	________
wonder	________
wander	________
stationery	________
stationary	________

Tip

Homophones are words that sound the same but are spelt differently.

Some sets of words aren't homophones but do sound alike.

lose/loose

Some sets of words aren't homophones but look alike.

wander/wonder

1 Underline the pairs that are homophones. Check your dictionary if you are unsure.

his/he's	your/you're
there/their	angel/angle
were/we're	their/they're
weather/whether	whose/who's

Tip

Mnemonics are memory tricks. They help you remember something more easily. look, blood

Here are some mnemonics: *Lose an **o** from loose.*

*I'd like a **pie**ce of **pie**.* *I'd like a **s**econd **s**erve of de**ss**ert.*

2 Which list words are homophones?

________ and ________ ________ and ________

3 Make up your own mnemonics. You can write or draw.

breath/breathe	practise/practice	wonder/wander

Spelling Rules! Student Book 4 (ISBN 9780655092704) © Janelle Ho, Helen Pearson

4 Write the correct word.

wonder wander	Walkers like to ____________ in the bush reserve. I ____________ what our new teacher will be like.
where were	This is ____________ Abdul hurt himself. He and his friends ____________ skateboarding when he fell.
lose loose	Ellen lets her puppies run ____________ in the garden. She has to be careful not to ____________ them.
desert dessert	Grandma makes the best chocolate ____________ . The largest ____________ in the world is the Sahara.

5 Write a word from Activity 1 in each space.

'Y__________ not watching TV till you tidy y__________ room!' Mum told Linda. Linda had no choice. 'W__________ shirt is this?' she asked. 'W__________ been messing up my room?'

'Hurry up, sis!' Brian grumbled. 'W__________ going to miss the show. Wonderboy will meet h__________ enemy and I bet h__________ in real trouble without Zappa. __________ such a great team!'

6 Write a sentence using both words.

whether
weather

____

____

____

bored
board

____

____

____

Reflection

- I can do this.
- I am not sure.
- I need help.

Unit 12 Revision

A cockroach can live up to ten days without a **head**, before dying of starvation.

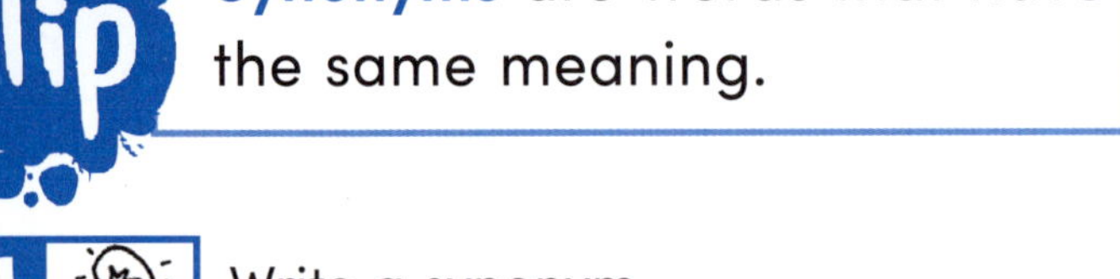

Tip: **Synonyms** are words that have the same meaning.

Tip: **Antonyms** are words that are opposite in meaning.

1 Write a synonym.

keen ____________
train ____________
nice ____________
place ____________
illness ____________
fixed ____________
continuous ____________

2 Write an antonym.

light ____________
behind ____________
introduction ____________
tight ____________
friend ____________
most ____________
accept ____________

3 Write the correct form of the verb to complete each sentence.

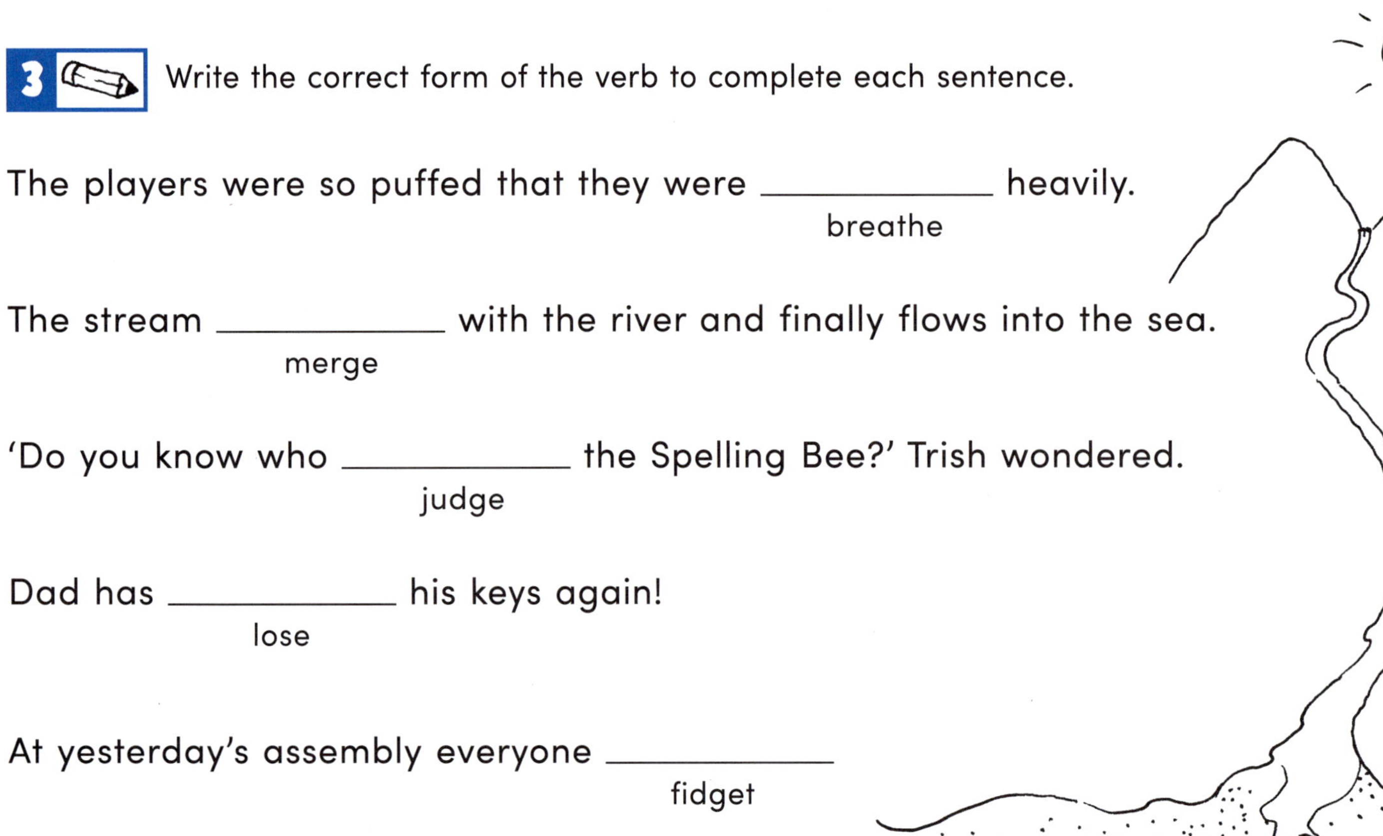

The players were so puffed that they were ____________ (breathe) heavily.

The stream ____________ (merge) with the river and finally flows into the sea.

'Do you know who ____________ (judge) the Spelling Bee?' Trish wondered.

Dad has ____________ (lose) his keys again!

At yesterday's assembly everyone ____________ (fidget) impatiently until the policeman ____________ (speak).

Spelling Rules! Student Book 4 (ISBN 9780655092704) © Janelle Ho, Helen Pearson

4 Write the words in the correct box.

eager and so invisible but jealous loose or

conjunction	adjective

5 Write the base word. Then write a sentence using either word.

separation ____________

____

stubbornness ____________

____

cleanliness ____________

____

6 Remove a letter from each word to make a new word. Colour the circle if the two words have different vowel sounds.

- ◯ close ____________
- ◯ breathe ____________
- ◯ least ____________
- ◯ dealt ____________
- ◯ meant ____________
- ◯ dessert ____________
- ◯ bridge ____________
- ◯ brain ____________

7 Fill in **ge**, **dge** or **j**.

While building the extension to our house, Dad hurt his knee with a sle_____hammer. The doctor gave him an in_____ection to help with the pain. Now he has two banda_____s and won't bu_____ from his chair.

Spelling Rules! Student Book 4 (ISBN 9780655092704) © Janelle Ho, Helen Pearson

Unit 13

Cat's eyes glow at night because they reflect light. This makes it easier for them to see in the dark.

Say Listen Look Understand Remember Practise

narrow	______
sorrow	______
tomorrow	______
loan	______
poach	______
coward	______
foul	______
announce	______
voucher	______
boundary	______
council	______
knowledge	______

1 Sort the list words according to the sound that **ow** makes.

rhymes with snow	rhymes with cow
______	______
______	______
______	______
______	______
______	______
	______

Which list word is the odd one out?

______

2 Change one letter at a time to make the first word into the last word.

moved
______
______
towel

prowl
______
______
frown

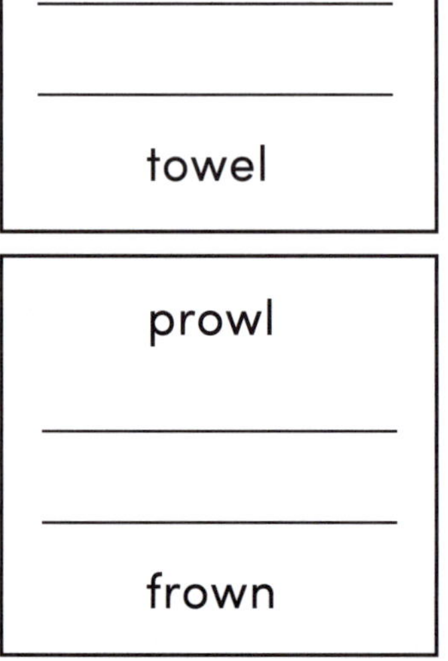

3 Use a suffix from the box to make a new word. Use each suffix only once.

ship	s	ing	ly	er	ful

prowl ______
power ______
announce ______
town ______
coward ______
boundary ______

Spelling Rules! Student Book 4 (ISBN 9780655092704) © Janelle Ho, Helen Pearson

4 Use the clues to complete the puzzle.

1	O	W				
2		O	W			
3			O	W		
4				O	W	
5					O	W

1. If a thing belongs to you, you are the ________.
2. Use this to dry yourself.
3. You might do this if you are angry.
4. give permission or let something happen
5. neither broad nor wide

5 There is an error in each sentence. Circle the incorrect word and write it correctly.

We are having pooched chicken for dinner. ________________

The councill is adding bicycle lanes to the main street. ________________

The voucher can be used from tommorrow. ________________

My favourite mystery books are out on lawn. ________________

The boundery between the houses is marked by a fence. ________________

6 *foul* and *fowl* are **homophones**. Use each word in a sentence.

foul ____

fowl ____

7 Write a compound word with **ow** for each picture.

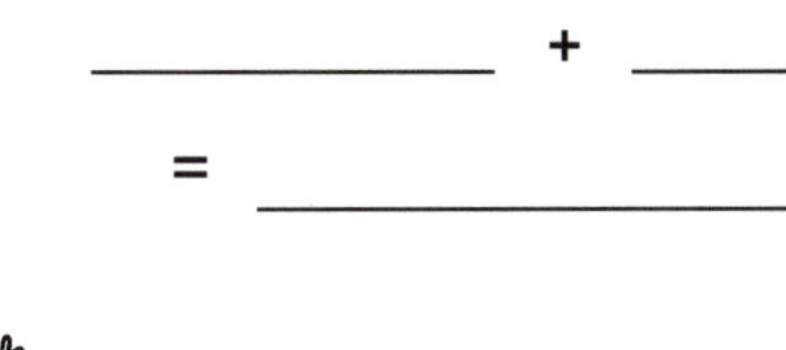

________ + ________ = ________________

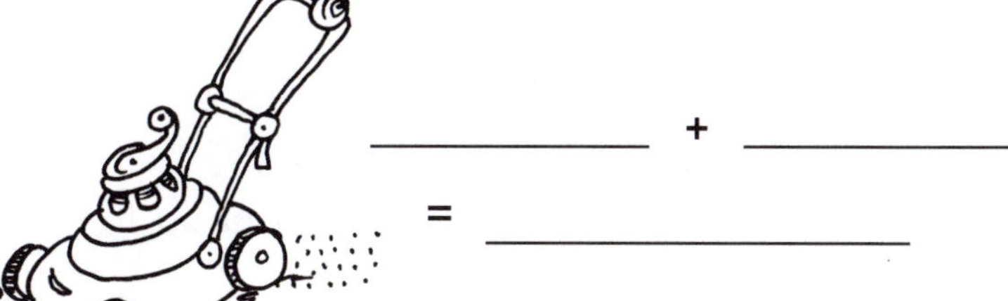

________ + ________ = ________________

8 Change one letter to change the vowel sound.

foul ____________ poach ____________

grown ____________ shore ____________

Reflection

- I can do this.
- I am not sure.
- I need help.

Unit 14

The size of an **ear**thquake is measured using a seismograph.

Say Listen Look Understand Remember Practise

verse ____________
superb ____________
alert ____________
convert ____________
deserve ____________
determined ____________
certain ____________
permanent ____________
earthquake ____________
research ____________
earnest ____________
rehearsal ____________

1 Write a list word that rhymes but is spelt differently.

purse ____________ perch ____________ curve ____________

2 Answer the questions.

Which two list words rhyme?

____________ ____________

Which list word has a prefix? ____________

3 Write list words in each category.

Parts of a text	Character traits	Verbs
chapter	serious	
stanza		

4 *Certainly* and *perhaps* express how sure we are about an event happening. Arrange these words in order, from most likely to least likely.

definitely not likely maybe certainly probably not

____

5 Write a list word. You may need to add a suffix.

Max ____________ his prize. His ____________ project not only included detailed information but also had great pictures. It was ____________.
His ____________ attitude to his work ____________ helped him.

Spelling Rules! Student Book 4 (ISBN 9780655092704) © Janelle Ho, Helen Pearson

6 Look at the words in the box. What does each prefix mean?

reverse return	research remarry	submerge submarine
re means ______________	**re** means ______________	**sub** means ______________

7 Use the clues to complete the puzzle.

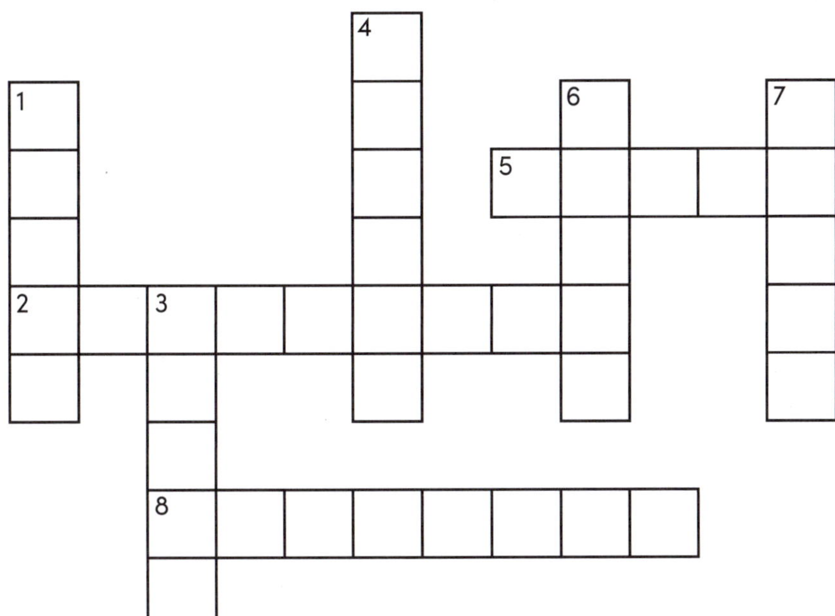

Down

1. attentive
3. past tense of hear
4. excellent
6. not late
7. first, second, ______________

Across

2. a practice for a performance
5. our planet
8. find out about something

8 Is the underlined word a verb, noun or adjective?

The ringing <u>alerted</u> us to leave the building immediately. ______________

After a good night's sleep, he awoke refreshed and <u>alert</u>. ______________

I did not do much <u>research</u> for my project. ______________

The scientists want to <u>research</u> more animals before they write their report. ______________

Mali is the most <u>determined</u> girl I know. ______________

The teachers <u>determine</u> where the students will sit in the classroom. ______________

Unit 15

The human intestine can stretch further than six metres!

Say Listen Look Understand Remember Practise

worthy	______
senior	______
surprise	______
further	______
burden	______
survive	______
journal	______
flavour	______
labour	______
courtesy	______
honour	______
nourish	______

1  Say each word. Circle the words that have the **er** sound.

forth	four	word
sour	colour	bored
course	worry	porch

2  Answer the questions.

Which list word has a silent letter? ______

Which list word has three syllables? ______

One list word begins with the letter that another ends with. Write the two list words.

______ ______

A **suffix** can:

- make a noun plural — *pen → pens   ox → oxen*
- change the tense of a verb — *walk → walked*
- make a new part of speech — *fair → fairly, fairness, fairest*

3 Add the suffix.

worth + y → ______

surprise + s → ______

surprise + ing + ly → ______

honour + ed → ______

honour + able → ______

survive + ed → ______

survive + al → ______

journal + ist → ______

nourish + es → ______

nourish + ment → ______

Spelling Rules! Student Book 4 (ISBN 9780655092704) © Janelle Ho, Helen Pearson

4 Add the prefix.

un + worthy → ________________

un + surprising → ________________

un + certain → ________________

un + natural → ________________

un + comfortable → ________________

dis + honour → ________________

dis + courtesy → ________________

dis + colour → ________________

dis + organised → ________________

dis + comfort → ________________

5 There is an error in each sentence. Circle the incorrect word and then write it correctly.

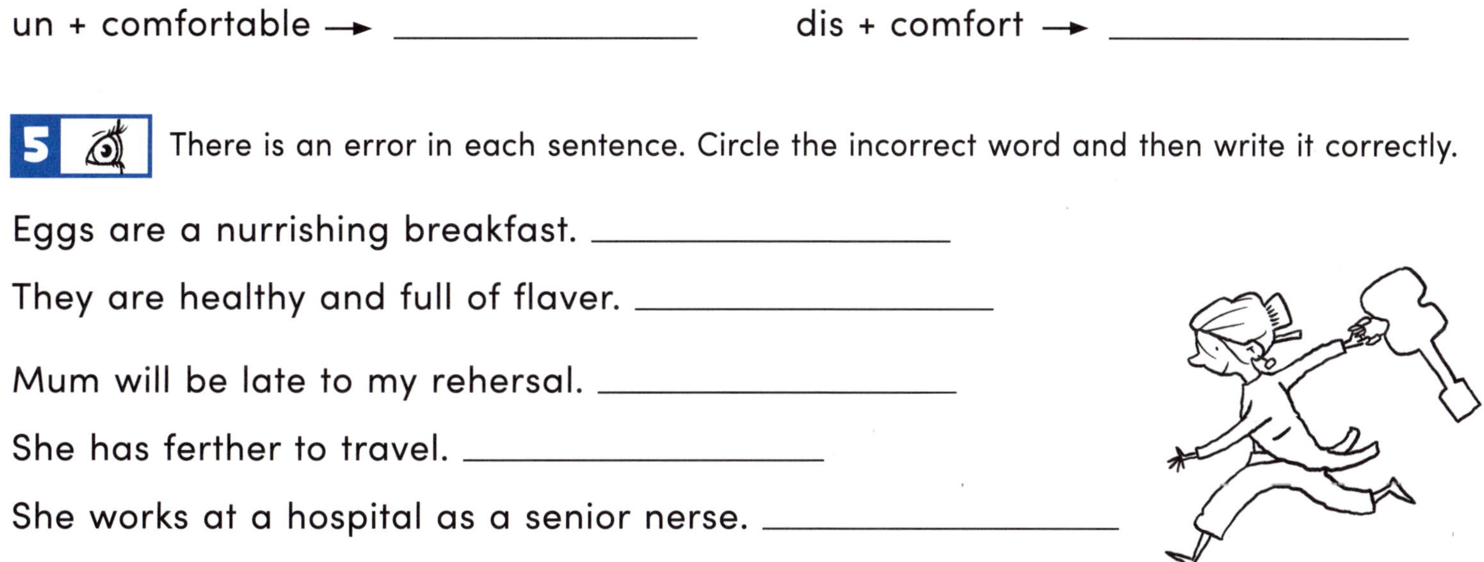

Eggs are a nurrishing breakfast. ________________

They are healthy and full of flaver. ________________

Mum will be late to my rehersal. ________________

She has ferther to travel. ________________

She works at a hospital as a senior nerse. ________________

Etymology is the study of the origin of words.
For example, *cricket* comes from an old French word *criquet*, meaning *stick*.

6 *Courtesy, courteous* and *courtship* all have the base word *court. This court is the court of a king.*
Use your dictionary to find the meaning of each word, then use it in your own sentence.

courtesy ________________________________

courteous ________________________________

courtship ________________________________

7 Answer the questions in full sentences.

What is your surname?

____

Which suburb do you live in?

____

Reflection

- I can do this.
- I am not sure.
- I need help.

Unit 16

Even though Mercury is the closest planet to the sun, its temperature can fall to –183 °C. That is much colder than it ever gets here on Earth!

Say Listen Look Understand Remember Practise	
nature	____________
future	____________
capture	____________
failure	____________
creature	____________
feature	____________
measure	____________
pleasure	____________
leisure	____________
adventure	____________
furniture	____________
temperature	____________

1 Write the words. Draw an arrow pointing to the word that has a different middle consonant sound.

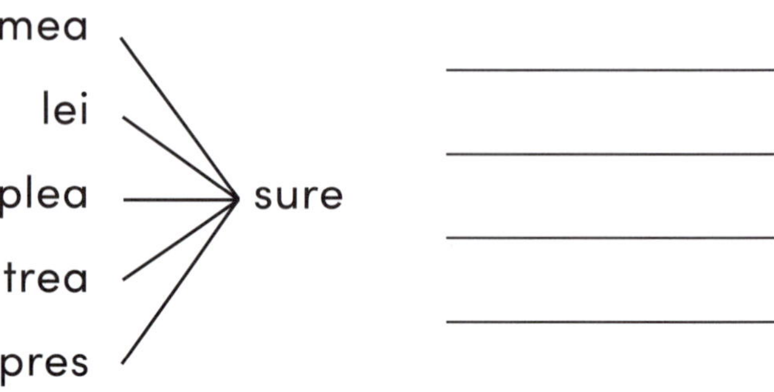

2 Write the words.

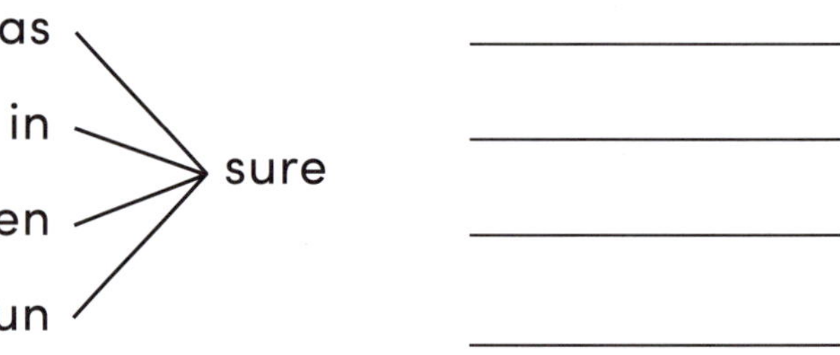

3 Add the prefix or suffix. Use the new word in a sentence. Use a dictionary if you need help.

leisure + ly → ____________

____

dis + pleasure → ____________

____

measure + ing → ____________

____

nature + al → ____________

____

4 Write the base words.

failure pleasure signature naturally impure

__________ __________ __________ __________ __________

5 Use each clue to write a word ending in **ure**. Only some are list words.

1. to heal, make well
2. sky blue colour
3. It may happen in the ________ .
4. time to do what you like
5. precious object
6. tables, chairs, beds

6 Write list words.

Week-long hikes in __________ reserves give my aunt and uncle a great deal of __________ .

The last time I had a fever my __________ rose to 39˚C.

My family played Monopoly by candlelight during the power__________ .

I wish I could have an __________ holiday on safari in Africa.

7 Answer the questions.

Temperature is measured with a thermometer.

thermo- is a word part from the Greek word *thermos*, which means __________ .

-meter is a word part from the Greek word *metron*, which means __________ .

Underwear that keeps you warm is known as __________ underwear.

The length of the outside of a shape is its __________ .

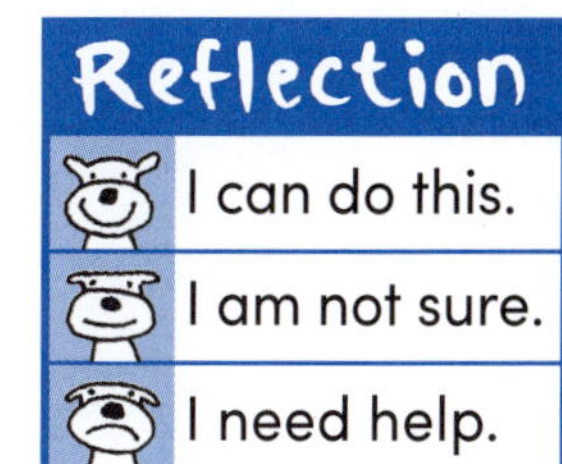

Unit 17

The colours of the rainbow are **r**ed, **o**range, **y**ellow, **g**reen, **b**lue, **i**ndigo and **v**iolet. When you want to remember it, think of Roy G Biv!

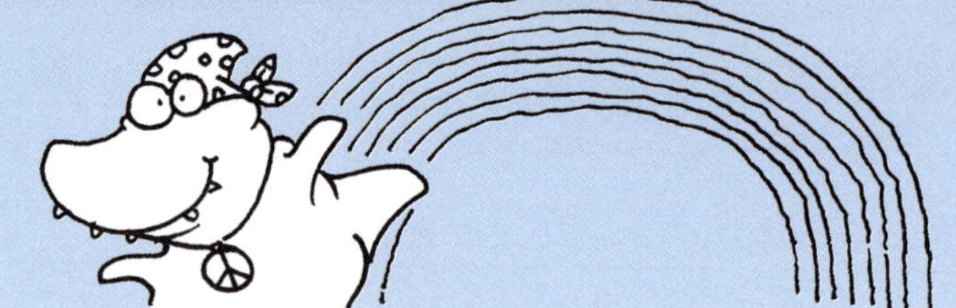

Say **L**isten **L**ook **U**nderstand **R**emember **P**ractise

ruby	______________
scarlet	______________
lilac	______________
violet	______________
emerald	______________
indigo	______________
crimson	______________
azure	______________
khaki	______________
ochre	______________
turquoise	______________
sapphire	______________

1 The names of colours often come from nature. Group the colour words from the list. Write the common name for each colour in the brackets. Use a dictionary to help you.

From flowers: ______________ (______________)

______________ (______________)

From gems: ______________ (______________)

______________ (______________)

______________ (______________)

______________ (______________)

From earth: ______________ (______________)

2 Think of other ways to group the colours. Use the space below to arrange your groups. Write a title for each group.

3 Use a dictionary to find words with *aqua*.

What does *aquamarine* mean? ______________________________

What does *aqua* mean? ______________________________

Write more words with *aqua*. ______________________________

Spelling Rules! Student Book 4 (ISBN 9780655092704) © Janelle Ho, Helen Pearson

4 Write a list word to describe each noun.

_____________ sky _____________ lips _____________ sea

_____________ land _____________ eyes _____________ blood

5 Use the clues to find a list word.

This colour has all the vowels except **a**. _____________

The first syllable of this colour is a mark left after you've hurt yourself. _____________

The word for this colour is Urdu in origin. _____________

Add one letter to *call* and rearrange the letters to make this colour. _____________

This colour is important to First Nations Australians. _____________

6 What do these expressions mean?

to feel blue _____________ to see red _____________

to be a black sheep _____________

a white elephant _____________

to have a green thumb _____________

a golden opportunity _____________

Tip

Similes compare one thing to another. They say that one thing is *like* another. *as red as a tomato* *as white as snow*

7 Make up your own similes.

as blue as _____________ as _____________ as _____________

as green as _____________ as _____________ as _____________

as yellow as _____________ as _____________ as _____________

as black as _____________ as _____________ as _____________

Reflection

I can do this.

I am not sure.

I need help.

Unit 18 Revision

A tree measured in 1780 had a circumference of 57.9 metres. It held the world record for a long time.

1 Write the plural.

coward ______________

journey ______________

machine ______________

ruby ______________

church ______________

rehearsal ______________

patient ______________

furniture ______________

knowledge ______________

boundary ______________

2 Complete the tables.

verb	add ed	add ing
poach		
allow		
alert		

verb	add ed	add ing
burden		
honour		
capture		

3 Add **er**, **ir**, **or**, **ur** or **ear** to complete each word.

Susu h____d yet another balloon b____st. She had already blown up th____ty but the wind knew no m____cy! She was conc____ned that by the time the last p____son arrived at her b____thday party, the only s____viv____s would be the balloons still in the packet.

4 Each sentence has one wrong word. Circle the word. Change one or more letters in the word to make a new word that fits the sentence.

I hope that in the feature, greenhouse gases won't be a problem. ______________

'Can you azure me that the leak can be fixed?' Dad asked the plumber. ______________

'I am curtain of that,' the plumber replied. ______________

I had to interview my grandparents as part of my rehearse for a project. ______________

The tigers look majestic as they frown in their enclosure. ______________

Spelling Rules! Student Book 4 (ISBN 9780655092704) © Janelle Ho, Helen Pearson

5 Write some unusual colour words for each of the common colours.

blue	green	red	yellow	brown

6 Make antonyms by adding a prefix.

certain ______________

usual ______________

honour ______________

please ______________

natural ______________

patient ______________

7 Make adverbs by adding the suffix **ly**.

narrow ______________

worth ______________

special ______________

certain ______________

usual ______________

earnest ______________

8 Use the clues to complete the puzzle. Write the hidden word.

1. good manners
2. a soft cloth for drying
3. a precious green stone
4. not ordinary
5. extremely old
6. the day after today
7. let or permit
8. all things not made by people
9. a long trip
10. an angry facial expression
11. maybe

Hidden word: ______________________

Unit 19

Ants have a lot of strength for their size. Some ants can drag objects that are 25 times their own weight.

Say Listen Look Understand Remember Practise	
fourth	______
fifth	______
eighth	______
ninth	______
twelfth	______
growth	______
warmth	______
length	______
strength	______
width	______
depth	______
breadth	______

Rule Most numbers add **th** to make the adjective form.

1 Write an adjective for each numeral.

1 ______ 2 ______

3 ______ 4 ______

5 ______ 6 ______

7 ______ 8 ______

9 ______ 10 ______

11 ______ 12 ______

2 Write two number adjectives that drop letters before adding **th**. Write the dropped letter or letters in the box.

______ ☐ ______ ☐

Rule Some words add **th** to make the noun form.

grow → growth

The vowel or vowels sometimes change too.

deep → depth

3 Add **th** to make the noun form.

warm ______ long ______ wide ______

true ______ strong ______ broad ______

young ______

Which nouns keep the vowels but sound different?

______

Spelling Rules! Student Book 4 (ISBN 9780655092704) © Janelle Ho, Helen Pearson

4 Fill in the missing adjectives.

If Monday is the first day of the week, Thursday is the ____________ day.

August is the ____________ month of the year.

The letter **i** is the ____________ letter of the alphabet.

On your ____________ birthday, you celebrate a decade of life.

Venus is the ____________ planet from the Sun.

A centenary celebration marks the ____________ year of an event.

5 Write a sentence about each shape. The first one is done for you.

oval — *Half of the oval is shaded.*

hexagon ____

pentagon ____

6 Write list words.

Use a ruler to measure the ____________ of wrapping paper you need.

Steel is a strong metal. Its ____________ makes it an ideal building material.

7 Describe a mythical creature with incredible strength.

____

____

8 *Fourth* and *forth* are **homophones**. Colour the correct word.

This is the | fourth | forth | time I've seen this movie.

The lion was pacing back and | fourth | forth | in his cage.

Unit 20

Lyrebirds are excellent mim**ic**s. They can imitate the sounds of other birds, animals, people and even chainsaws, horns and trains!

Meow

Say Listen Look Understand Remember Practise	
pan**ic**	________
picn**ic**	________
mag**ic**	________
log**ic**	________
crit**ic**	________
bas**ic**	________
mim**ic**	________
fantast**ic**	________
terrif**ic**	________
energet**ic**	________
automat**ic**	________
enthusiast**ic**	________

1 Write the list words in the correct group. Some words can be used more than once. Use a dictionary if you need help.

Verbs

____
____
____

Adjectives

____
____
____
____
____
____
____

Nouns

________ ________
________ ________
________ ________

2 Follow the pattern to add **ic**.

base + ic → basic

mime + ___ → ________

scene + ___ → ________

automate + ___ → ________

3 Write the adjective formed from the base word.

terrify → terrific

energy → ________

giant → ________

fantasy → ________

enthusiasm → ________

magnet → ________

drama → ________

tragedy → ________

Spelling Rules! Student Book 4 (ISBN 9780655092704) © Janelle Ho, Helen Pearson

s, **ed** and **ing** are verb suffixes. When you add **ed** and **ing** to a verb ending in **ic**, add a **k**. This keeps the hard **c** sound.

picnic → picnicked, picnicking

There is no change when **s** is added.

Add the suffix to each verb.

panic + ed → ______________ panic + ing → ______________

mimic + ed → ______________ mimic + ing → ______________

Colour the right word.

Eric loves summer. He usually | picnics | picnicks | with his family in the Botanic Gardens.

When the fire alarm sounded, there was no sign of | panic | panick |. It was only when we saw a rat that we | paniced | panicked |!

Julie is a good | mimic | mimick |. She's always | mimicing | mimicking | her classmates and teachers.

Write list words.

Bea used ______________ to solve the puzzle.

The players haven't stopped running yet. They're certainly very ______________.

My friends aren't ______________ about learning pottery. They'd rather paint.

Mowing the lawn is hard work! Wouldn't it be ______________ if someone invented an ______________ lawnmower?

You can download the ______________ app for free.

Write a list word that is a synonym.

reviewer ______________ imitate ______________

lively ______________ eager ______________

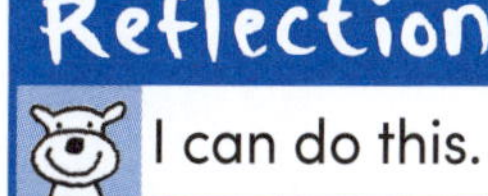

Spelling Rules! Student Book 4 (ISBN 9780655092704) © Janelle Ho, Helen Pearson

Unit 21

In winter, a snowshoe hare's fur changes from brown to white, so that predators have trouble seeing it against the snow. Now, that's a survival trick!

Say Listen Look Understand Remember Practise

capit**al**	____________
hospit**al**	____________
fin**al**	____________
logic**al**	____________
magic**al**	____________
nation**al**	____________
natur**al**	____________
digit**al**	____________
crimin**al**	____________
critic**al**	____________
surviv**al**	____________
emotion**al**	____________

1 Add **al** to the base word to make a list word.

magic → ____________

nation → ____________

nature → ____________

survive → ____________

arrive → ____________

2 Write the base words. Use a dictionary if you need help.

logical ____________

emotional ____________

criminal ____________

personal ____________

Tip Adding **al** to a word usually changes it to an adjective. Some words ending in **al** are both nouns and adjectives.

3 Write list words that are nouns. Put an asterisk next to the ones that can also be adjectives.

____________ ____________ ____________ ____________ ____________

Choose one word. Write a sentence for each usage.

Noun: ____________

Adjective: ____________

4 Write words ending in **al**.

to do with your teeth ____________

to do with your body ____________

to do with your mind ____________

to do with your spine ____________

Spelling Rules! Student Book 4 (ISBN 9780655092704) © Janelle Ho, Helen Pearson

5 Draw lines or shapes to match each label.

vertical | horizontal | diagonal | symmetrical

6 Rearrange the letters to make an **al** word that completes each sentence.

The Danish __________ (oyral) family lives in Copenhagen, the __________ (tapical) city of Denmark.

The __________ (caoll) shops hold a street market once a month.

Dogs are good pets because they are __________ (alloy).

An avatar is a __________ (glaidit) person in a computer game.

Regular __________ (cailshyp) exercise is both fun and healthy.

With the internet, we live in a __________ (bollag) village.

Tip Etymology is the study of the origins and development of words.

7 The word *final* comes from the Latin word *finis,* which means *limit* or *boundary.* Use a dictionary to find the meanings of these related words.

finish ____________________

finite ____________________

define ____________________

definite ____________________

8 Make a mnemonic to help you remember how to spell *definite.*

Reflection

- I can do this.
- I am not sure.
- I need help.

Unit 22

Some experts say that at least one **thousand** million grams of space dust rain down on Earth every day.

Say Listen Look Understand Remember Practise

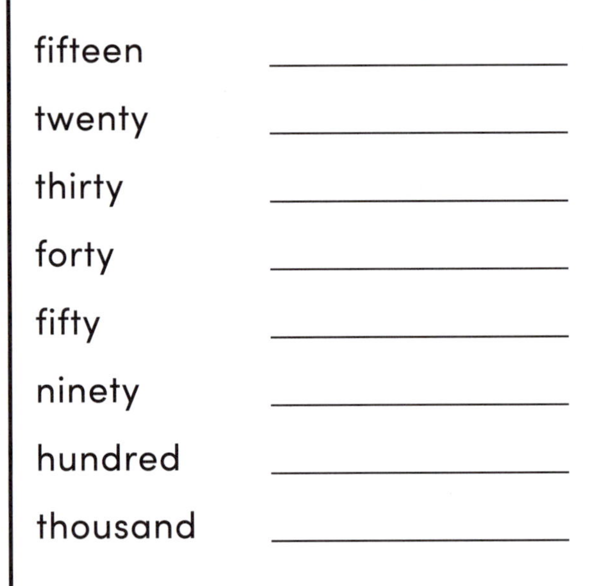

eleven	______
twelve	______
thirteen	______
fourteen	______
fifteen	______
twenty	______
thirty	______
forty	______
fifty	______
ninety	______
hundred	______
thousand	______

1 Write a list word for each numeral.

11 ______ 12 ______

13 ______ 15 ______

20 ______ 40 ______

Tip Numbers from 13 to 19 end in **teen**.

2 Add **teen** to these numbers.

14 four + teen → ______

16 ____ + teen → ______

17 seven + ____ → ______

18 eight + ____ → ______

19 ____ + ____ → ______

3 Write the numbers in words. Circle the part of the word that is the same for each pair.

13 ______	15 ______	12 ______	18 ______
30 ______	50 ______	20 ______	80 ______

4 Write the word for the number.

90	100	1000	1 000 000
______	______	______	______

Tip Numbers ending in 0 between 20 and 90 end in **ty**.

5 Cross out the letter that is left out when **ty** is added. Write the word and the numeral.

four + ty → ______ ____ eight + ty → ______ ____

Spelling Rules! Student Book 4 (ISBN 9780655092704) © Janelle Ho, Helen Pearson

Numbers between 21 and 99 that are not multiples of 10 need a hyphen.
twenty-one *sixty-five* *eighty-nine*

Write the word for the numeral.

33 ________ 44 ________ 81 ________
57 ________ 28 ________ 99 ________
65 ________ 72 ________ 46 ________

To make a number into an adjective, **th** is usually added.
Numbers that end in **ty** change **y** to **i** and add **eth**.
twenty → twentieth *sixty → sixtieth*

Write the adjective for each numeral.

7 ________ 10 ________ 14 ________
30 ________ 40 ________ 50 ________
21 ________ 82 ________ 75 ________

8 Write a number word to complete each sentence.

My mum is ________ years old and my dad is ________ years old.

________ years is the same as five decades.

Two dozen is the same as ________.

Some people believe Friday the ________ is an unlucky day.

There are one ________ years in a century.

There are one ________ years in a millennium.

Unit 23

If a cat has hair standing up on its body and tail and its back is arched, watch out – it's aggressive!

Say Listen Look Understand Remember Practise

accept ______
accuse ______
attempt ______
attitude ______
pollute ______
approach ______
disappoint ______
opportunity ______
necessary ______
recommend ______
occasion ______
aggressive ______

1 Add a suffix from the box to each base word.

ance	ion	tion	ly	ment	al

accept ______
pollute ______
embarrass ______
appear ______
occasion ______
disappoint ______
accuse ______
necessary ______
recommend ______

Rule **g** and **c** make their soft sound when they are followed by **e** or **i**.

2 Circle the word in each pair that includes a soft consonant sound.

suggest	aggressive	accent	recount
accuse	accept	occasion	accident

3 These sentences have too many double letters. Rewrite each sentence correctly.

I've allways bellieved that ice cream is neccessarry for good health.

______

There's a speccial occassion this Saturday. It's Grandpa's seventty-fifth birthday!

______

4 Add a prefix to make an antonym.

_____ + appear → _______________ _____ + necessary → _______________

5 Add a suffix to make the correct form of the verb.

The lights turned red as I _______________. (approach)

I _______________ Nina of taking my cap but in fact I had left it at home. (accuse)

Tomorrow the principal is _______________ who the school captain will be. (announce) I think it will be Cassie because she _______________ all the right qualities. (possess)

You are _______________ me! (embarrass)

Tip

Except and **accept** are often confused.
except = not including *accept* = take or receive
Affect and **effect** are also often confused.
affect = to cause a change in something *effect* = a result

6 Write the correct words to complete each sentence.

accept
except

Everyone in the family _______________ her grandmother was in the hall to see Ellen _______________ her award.

affect
effect

The things we do _______________ the environment. Pollution has a long-lasting _______________.

7 Use the clues to write a list word.

Which word has a harbour in it? _______________

Which word has a survey in it? _______________

Which word has a synonym for repair? _______________

Which word has a dot in it? _______________

Reflection

- I can do this.
- I am not sure.
- I need help.

Adults have around five **million** hairs all over their bodies – that's about the same number as a gorilla!

1 Write the missing words.

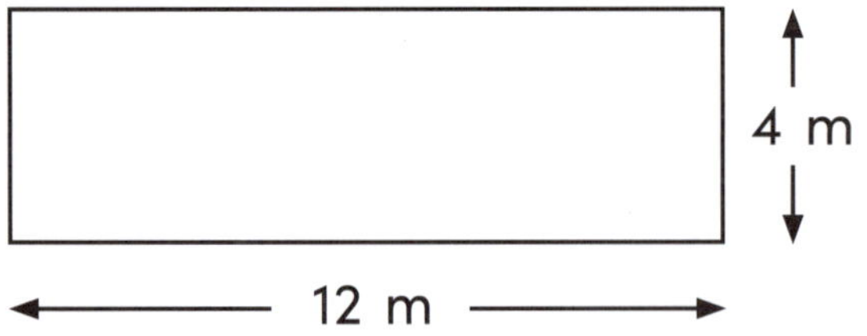

(Rectangle: 12 m long, 4 m high)

The __________ of the rectangular garden is 12 metres.

Its __________ is 4 metres.

The breadth of something is the same as its __________.

2 Write a number word or number adjective to complete each sentence.

There are __________ letters in the English alphabet, of which __________ are consonants. The __________ letter is a and the __________ one is e.

There are three __________ and __________ days in a leap year. A year is divided into __________ months. August, the __________ month, has __________ days.

3 Write an adjective by adding **al**.

magic	nation	emotion	survive
__________	__________	__________	__________

4 Write double consonants to complete each word.

a___roach	a___use	po___e___	su___est	emba___a___
a___ounce	a___ear	sa___hire	pre___ure	tomo___ow

5 Use each word in a sentence.

accept ______________________________

except ______________________________

Spelling Rules! Student Book 4 (ISBN 9780655092704) © Janelle Ho, Helen Pearson

6 Use the clues to complete the puzzle.

	1								
2									
	3								
		4							
	5								
	6								
	7								
		8							

1. The ambulance took her to the _____
2. It's great! It's _____!
3. A heater provides _____ when it's cold.
4. You win silver if you come _____.
5. After ninety-nine comes one _____.
6. Something that makes sense is _____.
7. At assembly, we sang the _____ anthem.
8. There are _____ days in April.

Ants have great ____________________ for their size.

7 Replace the underlined word or words with a more interesting list word you have learnt. Rewrite the sentence using the correct form of the new word.

Jenny <u>really wants</u> to go to the circus.

____

Grandpa has a watch that winds <u>without him having to do it</u>.

____

If you <u>go near</u> their babies, animals will <u>act as if they want to fight</u>.

____

8 Write the correct form of the word to complete each sentence.

Mr Chang ____________ (panic) when he ____________ (realise) he had lost his keys.

Grandma always ____________ (embarrass) Dad by telling stories of his childhood.

Touch football has only a few ____________ (base) rules.

Unit 25

The average Australian eats around 6 kilograms of chocolate each year. That's a lot of Easter eggs!

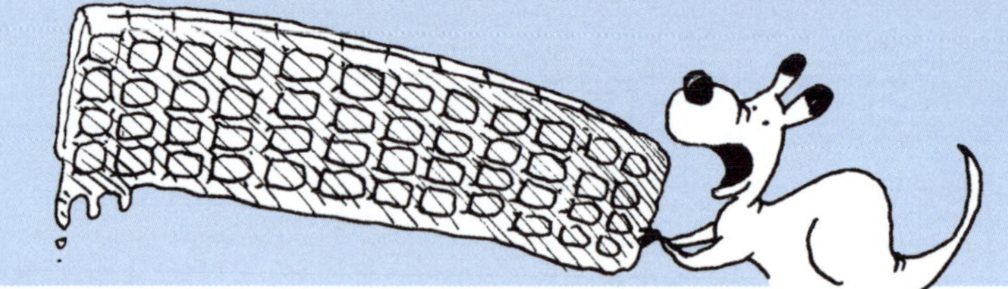

Say Listen Look Understand Remember Practise

ginger	____________
gently	____________
general	____________
average	____________
generous	____________
religion	____________
intelligent	____________
fragile	____________
generation	____________
advantage	____________
emergency	____________
gymnasium	____________

1 Circle the letter **g** if it has a soft sound.

danger	regret	germ
eager	gigantic	logical

2 Fill in the missing vowels to make words with a soft **g** sound.

man _ g _

_ rr _ ng _

_ xyg _ n

eng _ n _ _ r

g _ psy

p _ ss _ ng _ r

_ r _ g _ n _ l

3 Group the list words as nouns, adjectives and adverbs. Use a dictionary if you need help. (Three words can be used as both nouns and adjectives.)

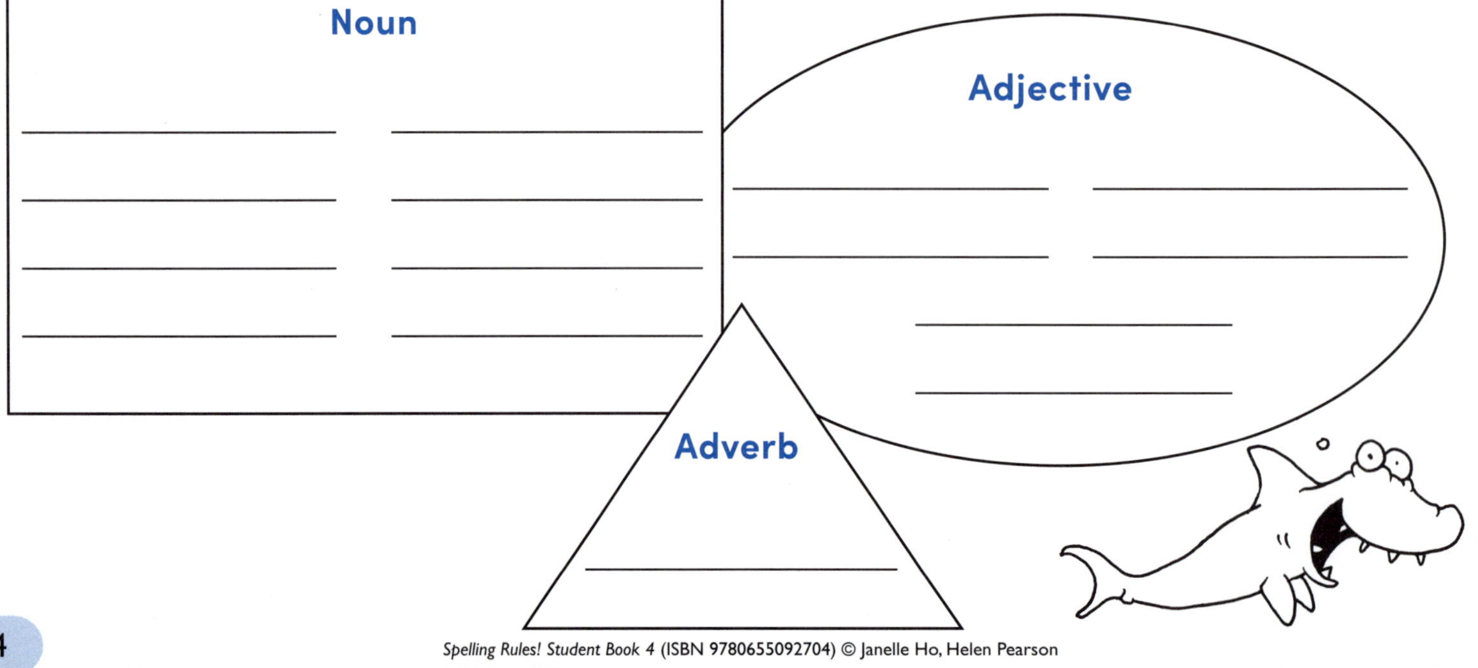

Spelling Rules! Student Book 4 (ISBN 9780655092704) © Janelle Ho, Helen Pearson

4 Add **ly** to make adverbs.

generous ________________ intelligent ________________

general ________________ gentle ________________

5 Make antonyms by adding **dis** or **un** as a prefix.

intelligent ________________ advantage ________________ original ________________

6 Choose the correct word to complete each sentence.

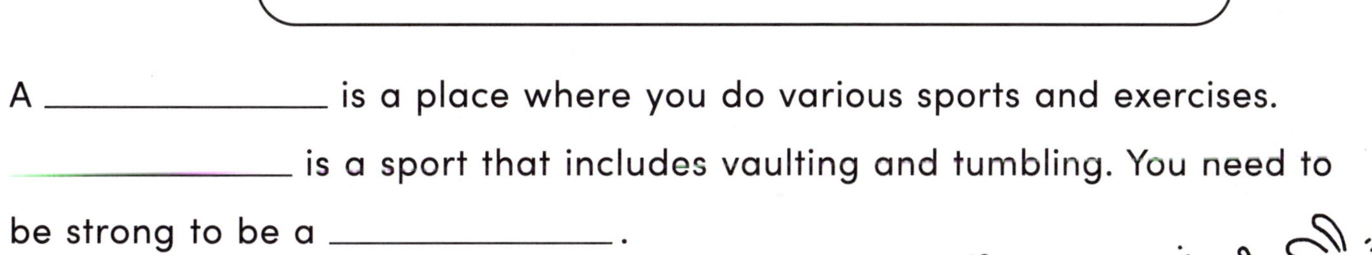

gymnast	gymnastics	gymnasium

A ________________ is a place where you do various sports and exercises.

________________ is a sport that includes vaulting and tumbling. You need to be strong to be a ________________.

7 Circle the word or words that do not make sense.
Write a list word that you could use instead.

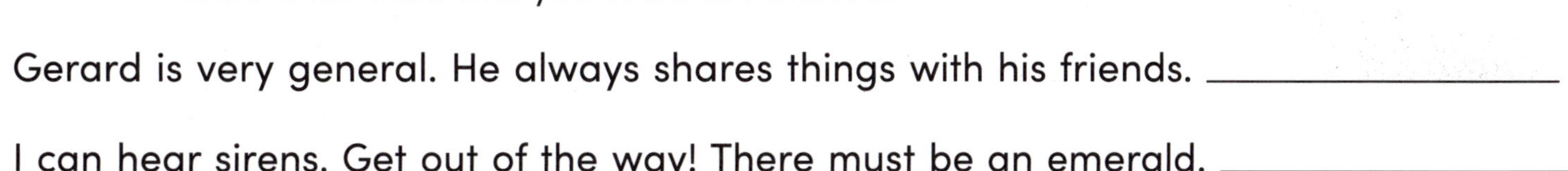

Gerard is very general. He always shares things with his friends. ________________

I can hear sirens. Get out of the way! There must be an emerald. ________________

Angie has an adverb because she's played this game before. ________________

Our generator will be the first to live mainly in a digital world. ________________

8 Write an antonym that has a soft **g** sound.

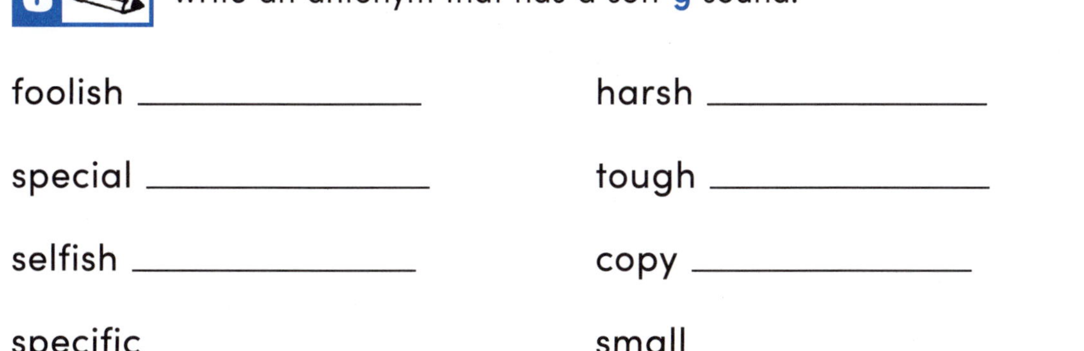

foolish ________________ harsh ________________

special ________________ tough ________________

selfish ________________ copy ________________

specific ________________ small ________________

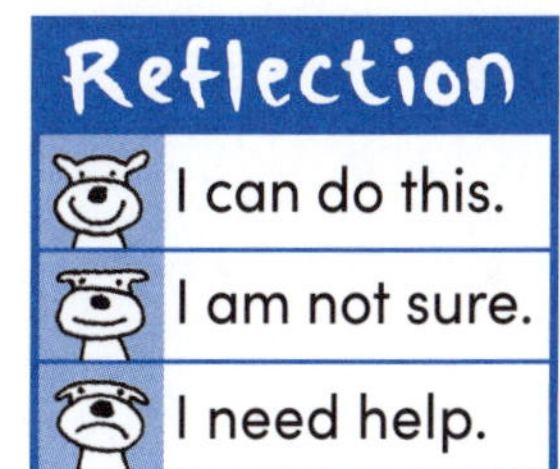

Spelling Rules! Student Book 4 (ISBN 9780655092704) © Janelle Ho, Helen Pearson

Unit 26

A skunk will spray you with very smelly liquid if you make it nerv**ous**!

Say **L**isten **L**ook **U**nderstand **R**emember **P**ractise

seri**ous**	________
preci**ous**	________
delici**ous**	________
fam**ous**	________
nerv**ous**	________
danger**ous**	________
courage**ous**	________
furi**ous**	________
cauti**ous**	________
envi**ous**	________
spaci**ous**	________
vari**ous**	________

1 Write the list word that comes from the same word family.

vary ________

courage ________

space ________

fame ________

danger ________

envy ________

nerve ________

fury ________

caution ________

deliciously ________

seriousness ________

2 Colour the correct word.

Words that end in **ous** are | adjectives | nouns | adverbs |.

When the base word ends in silent **e**, drop the **e** before adding **ous**.

fame → famous

If the base word ends in **ce**, change the **e** to **i** before adding **ous**.

space → spacious

3 Make an adjective by adding the suffix **ous**.

adventure → ________

grace → ________

ridicule → ________

vice → ________

Spelling Rules! Student Book 4 (ISBN 9780655092704) © Janelle Ho, Helen Pearson

If the base word ends in **ge**, keep the **e** when adding **ous** to keep the **g** sound soft. *courage* → *courageous*

4 Make an adjective by adding the suffix **ous**.

outrage → ______________ advantage → ______________

If the base word ends in **y**, change **y** to **i** before adding **ous**.
envy → *envious* *vary* → *various*

5 Make an adjective by adding the suffix **ous**.

fury → ______________ mystery → ______________

glory → ______________ luxury → ______________

6 Write list words.

Recently I watched a program about a ______________ athlete. She had suffered a ______________ accident, which caused her to lose both legs. However, she was very ______________. She overcame her disability to represent her country in the Paralympic Games. In an interview, she said that she still felt ______________ and had butterflies in her stomach before each race. The medals she has won at the Games and in other competitions are among her most ______________ possessions.

7 Write list words.

A person who is well-known is ______________.

A person who is extremely angry is ______________.

A person who doesn't take risks is ______________.

A person who wants what someone else has is ______________.

Food that people want to eat is ______________.

An activity that is unsafe is ______________.

Unit 27

The average person can only memorise 7 digits. You can increase that by using an mnemonic.

Say Listen Look Understand Remember Practise

lessen	______
stiffen	______
toughen	______
sadden	______
awaken	______
straighten	______
finalise	______
memorise	______
fantasise	______
energise	______
sympathise	______
visualise	______

en changes an adjective to a verb.

1 Write the list words as base word + **en**.

lessen → less + ______

stiffen → ______ + en

toughen → ______ + ______

sadden → ______ + ______

awaken → ______ + ______

straighten → ______ + ______

2  Add **en**. Remember to apply your spelling rules.

fast ______ short ______

light ______ shake ______

flat ______ quick ______

deaf ______ rot ______

ise changes a noun to a verb.

3 Write the list word that is from the same word family.

final ______ memory ______ energy ______ visual ______

State the spelling rule for words ending in **y**.

______

4  Add **ise**.

fantasy ______ sympathy ______ summary ______

Spelling Rules! Student Book 4 (ISBN 9780655092704) © Janelle Ho, Helen Pearson

5 Write a list word to complete each sentence. You may need to add a suffix.

Dad found Tony ________________ the pet cat's tail.

Grandma was ________________ to learn of her friend's illness.

I love to ________________ about what it would be like to live in space.

We love where we live because we are ________________ every morning by birdsong.

Mum has an ________________ cold shower after work.

6 Answer the questions.

What is a homophone of lessen? ________________

What is an antonym of lessen? ________________

What is a synonym of lessen? ________________

7 The word *memory* comes from the Latin word *memor*, which means *mindful*. Write the meanings of these related words. Use a dictionary if you need help.

memory ________________

memorise ________________

memorial ________________

remember ________________

8 A mnemonic is a memory trick to help you remember something difficult. Write or draw a mnemonic for a list word or a rule.

Reflection

- I can do this.
- I am not sure.
- I need help.

Unit 28

The first water treat**ment** happened in the 1700s. People used wool, sponge and charcoal.

Say Listen Look Understand Remember Practise

move**ment**	________
state**ment**	________
argu**ment**	________
amaze**ment**	________
measure**ment**	________
govern**ment**	________
environ**ment**	________
treat**ment**	________
develop**ment**	________
attach**ment**	________
encourage**ment**	________
disappoint**ment**	________

Tip **ment** changes a verb to a noun.

1 Write the list words as base word + **ment**.

treatment → treat + ________
development → ________ + ment
attachment → ________ + ________
movement → ________ + ________
statement → ________ + ________
amazement → ________ + ________
government → ________ + ________
measurement → ________ + ________
encouragement → ________ + ________
disappointment → ________ + ________
environment → ________ + ________

2 Say each list word. Write the words that match the number of syllables.

2 syllables

____
____
____

4 syllables

____
____
____
____

3 Add suffixes to **move**.

move + s ________
move + ed ________
move + ing ________
move + er ________
move + ment ________

Which spelling rule does not apply when **s** and **ment** are added? Why not?

____
____

Spelling Rules! Student Book 4 (ISBN 9780655092704) © Janelle Ho, Helen Pearson

4 Each group of words forms a category. Write a list word for each category and add more examples.

Category	Examples
______________	minister, parliament, MP, ____________, ____________
______________	hours, metres, grams, ____________, ____________
______________	erosion, recycling, pollution, ____________, ____________

5 Write a list word that is a synonym.

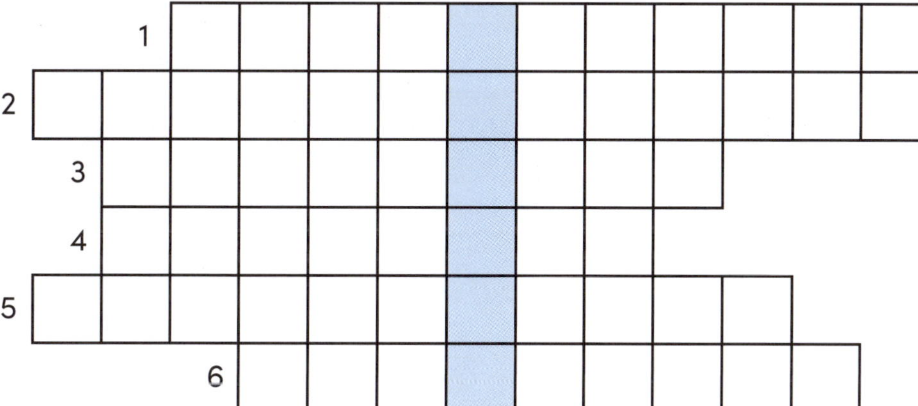

1. growth
2. cheer
3. care
4. quarrel
5. surroundings
6. declaration

Hidden word: ______________________

Prefixes and suffixes are types of affixes.

6 Add as many affixes as you can.

move: ____

treat: ____

develop: ____

7 The words *amazement* and *disappointment* describe feelings. Describe a time when you felt one of these feelings.

____

____

____

____

____

Unit 29

Australia's first computer weighed about 2 tonnes and used 3000 times more electricity than modern computers – but was around 500 000 times slower!

Say Listen Look Understand Remember Practise

computer	______
laptop	______
email	______
internet	______
mobile	______
keyboard	______
program	______
icon	______
download	______
insert	______
delete	______
barcode	______

1 Write the list word for each picture.

92765

______ ______ ______

2 What are these symbols called?

* ______ / ______

______ & ______

3 Write the full names for these keyboard keys.

fn ______ alt ______

esc ______ del ______

Tip

Compound words are two whole words joined together to form a new word.

soft + ware → software

4 Use a dictionary to find the meaning of *ware*.

ware = ______

Write another computer compound word that ends in *ware*. ______

5 Write the list words that are compound words.

______ ______ ______ ______

6 The same object may have different names in different countries. A mobile phone is also called a cellphone or a handphone. Use the internet to find out which countries use each word.

cellphone ______ handphone ______

Spelling Rules! Student Book 4 (ISBN 9780655092704) © Janelle Ho, Helen Pearson

Many terms or phrases are abbreviated to the first letter of each word.
IT = **i**nformation **t**echnology

7 Unscramble the letters to make the full name for each abbreviation.

PC aspolner pertumoc ______________________________

WWW olwrd diew wbe ______________________________

GB ygabgesti ______________________________

USB lunarvise ariels usb ______________________________

URL omufrni reecrosu rocatol ______________________________

8 The names of some countries and states are commonly abbreviated. Write the full name for each abbreviation.

NZ ______________________________ HK ______________________________

UK ______________________________ USA ______________________________

NY ______________________________ ACT ______________________________

9 Abbreviations are sometimes used in email, text messages and on websites. Write the full text for each abbreviation.

LOL ______________________________ ASAP ______________________________

BTW ______________________________ FAQ ______________________________

10 Write the correct form of a list word to complete each sentence.

I spend time every afternoon ______________ my cousin overseas.

______________ help managers check the goods in their stores.

Our computer at home is ______________ so that Mum and Dad can check what we're using it for.

______________ big files from the internet can take a long time.

Oh no! I think I've accidentally ______________ the research I did on dolphins.

Reflection

	I can do this.
	I am not sure.
	I need help.

Spelling Rules! Student Book 4 (ISBN 9780655092704) © Janelle Ho, Helen Pearson

Murphy the donkey was given the Purple Cross in honour of all the courage**ous** donkeys that carried wounded troops at Gallipoli.

 **1** Circle the soft **c** or **g** sounds. Underline the hard **c** or **g** sounds.

ginger circle garage gigantic success cyclone

 **2** Make compound words by using one word from each box.

key	lap	down	soft	bar
ware	load	board	code	top

________ ________ ________ ________ ________

 **3** Write the adjective form of the word by adding **y** or **ous**.

sag winter danger vary courage

________ ________ ________ ________ ________

4 Replace the underlined words with one word. Rewrite the sentence.

Mr Smit can't open the <u>document that I added</u> to my email.

____

Filipo hates it when we have a <u>situation when we don't get along</u>.

____

Be careful! The vase is <u>easily broken</u>.

____

I don't just daydream, I <u>use my imagination to think up unrealistic ideas</u>.

____

Being tall <u>helps a player</u> in ball games like netball and volleyball.

____

Spelling Rules! Student Book 4 (ISBN 9780655092704) © Janelle Ho, Helen Pearson

 Write a word ending in **ous** to describe each character.

Pedro always wants to find out more about things. He is ________________.

Janet is feeling ________________ about having to welcome the visitor.

My dog Max gets very ________________ whenever I play with my cat.

When Lara discovered her sister had been secretly reading her emails, she was ________________.

John has appeared in many television commercials. He is now ________________.

6 Circle the word that does not make sense in each sentence. Write the correct word.

Ian's been training for the competition sincere the summer. ________________

Don't forget to delete the address or the email can't be sent. ________________

We need to lesson the amount of salt and sugar we eat. ________________

I have to message all the spelling words for tomorrow's test. ________________

Rita symphonies with me because she has lost her pet before. Unluckily, it was found.

________________ ________________

7 Proofread this text. The text has five words that are incorrect. Circle the mistakes. Then write the correct spelling of the words in the boxes.

Janice is a computer genious. Resently she took part in a competition to write a proggram. Although she didn't win, she did better than avrage. When she was interviewed for our school newsletter, she said it was important to have a logical sisterm, a scientific approach and good organisation.

Unit 31

It is impossible to fold a piece of paper of almost any size in half more than seven times. Try it!

Say Listen Look Understand Remember Practise	
niece	________
belief	________
achieve	________
alien	________
receipt	________
deceive	________
protein	________
weird	________
reign	________
seize	________
beige	________
feisty	________

1 Circle the words that don't have an **ee** sound (as in *see*).

weight	foreign	deceive
relieve	weird	reign
seize	fierce	achieve
sleigh	protein	alien

Rule

The general rule is **i** before **e** except after **c**.

BUT some words do not follow this rule.

2 Write the list words that don't follow the rule.

________ ________ ________

________ ________ ________

3 Fill in **ie** or **ei**.

bel___ve rec___ve ach___ve

w___rd h___ght c___ling

4 Write the correct word to complete each sentence.

beliefs
believes

Mr Johnson ____________ that UFOs have visited Earth.

It is important to respect other people's ____________.

relief
relieve

If you burn your skin, use cool water to ____________ the pain.

When the lost girl found her parents, she cried with ____________.

Spelling Rules! Student Book 4 (ISBN 9780655092704) © Janelle Ho, Helen Pearson

 Write a sentence using each word.

receipt	______________________________
receive	______________________________

 Draw a line to match each word with its meaning. If you need help, use a dictionary.

niece	vain or having a high opinion of yourself
foreign	mislead or trick
conceited	from another country
perceive	discover using one of your five senses
deceive	what a girl is to her aunt and uncle

7 One word in each sentence is missing the letter **e**. Find the word, fill in the missing **e** and write the word correctly.

My parents encourage me to size every opportunity to learn. ______________

Mr Yang has bought his nice Emma a necklace for Christmas. ______________

Janet was relived to discover her precious pet was safe. ______________

The foal will take a while to train because she is fisty. ______________

We must have clean hands at Grandpa's because the furniture is big. ______________

Rain, **rein** and **reign** are homophones.
rain = wet weather   *rein* = a strap to lead a horse   *reign* = royal rule

 Colour the correct word.

Queen Elizabeth I of England never married during her long | rain | rein | reign |.

Use the | rains | reins | reigns | gently but firmly.

Heavy | rain | rein | reign | filled our new water tank.

Spelling Rules! Student Book 4 (ISBN 9780655092704) © Janelle Ho, Helen Pearson

Unit 32

Cheetahs are **ex**tremely fast over short distances. They can reach 100 km/h when chasing prey.

Say **L**isten **L**ook **U**nderstand **R**emember **P**ractise

exist	____________
exchange	____________
examination	____________
explosion	____________
expensive	____________
exaggerate	____________
excursion	____________
exceed	____________
except	____________
extinct	____________
exhausted	____________
exhibition	____________

1 Which **c** is the odd one out? Circle it.

excite excuse exercise except

Explain your choice.

____

Use this word in a sentence.

____

____

2 What does the letter **X** stand for in each example?

Xmas ____________

on a map ____________

at the end of a letter ____________

on the face of a clock ____________

3 Use one syllable from each column to form list words.

ex	cel	sive
	er	tion
	pen	ly
	treme	lent
	am	cise
	tinc	ple

____________ ____________

____________ ____________

____________ ____________

Write the word with a double consonant again.

____

4 Write the list words that have a silent letter.

____________ ____________

5 How many words can you make using the letters from these list words? Write words that are three, four or five letters long. Give yourself one point for each word, then a bonus point for each word that includes the letter **x**.

explain	exaggerate	exhausted	expensive

points: ______ points: ______ points: ______ points: ______

6 Add suffixes to these words.

	explain	exaggerate	exercise	exceed
add **ed**				
add **ing**				

7 Write the correct form of the word **excite** in each space.

Rahman was going to Malaysia with his family to visit his relatives. I had never seen him so ____________ before. This was his first time on an aeroplane and the first time he would see his cousins. I guess that is quite ____________!

Tip **Anagrams** are words that have the same letters arranged in a different order. For example, *red raw* is an anagram of *drawer*.

8 Write a list word that is an anagram.

expect ______________ exits ______________ spoil oxen ______________

9 Write the correct form of list words.

Some people claim the rate of ____________ for some plant and animal species is ____________. I would be ____________ happy if that were true.

Reflection

- I can do this.
- I am not sure.
- I need help.

Unit 33

Several centuries ago, **barbers** also did the work of surgeons and dentists.

Say Listen Look Understand Remember Practise

author	______
grocer	______
carpenter	______
lawyer	______
assistant	______
accountant	______
electrician	______
politician	______
journalist	______
pharmacist	______
chef	______
pilot	______

1 Use the picture as a clue for each occupation.

______ ______ ______

______ ______ ______

News

______ ______ ______

The names of occupations are often base words with a suffix added.

wait + er → waiter *serve + ant → servant*

music + ian → musician *art + ist → artist*

2 Write the base word.

lawyer ______ assistant ______

engineer ______ politician ______

journalist ______ conductor ______

physiotherapist ______ farmer ______

scientist ______ pharmacist ______

builder ______ actor ______

Spelling Rules! Student Book 4 (ISBN 9780655092704) © Janelle Ho, Helen Pearson

 Each word has the wrong ending. Write each word correctly.

docter ______________	photographist ______________
magicist ______________	dentant ______________
instructant ______________	drivor ______________
accountist ______________	electricant ______________

Apostrophes can be used to show who something belongs to. In other words, apostrophes can show **possession**.

the pilot's suitcase (one pilot + one suitcase)

the pilot's duties (one pilot + more than one duty)

When the owner is plural, the apostrophe comes **after** the plural. When the plural ends in **s**, do not add a second **s** after the apostrophe.

the pilots' uniforms (more than one pilot + more than one uniform)

the children's toys (more than one child + more than one toy)

 Add the missing apostrophes. Circle the words where the apostrophe does not show possession.

I needed a present for my friends birthday, so I thought Id look in Mr and Mrs Tangs new bookshop. Its called The Reading Room. It was crowded but I could tell from the customers smiles that they were enjoying themselves. The displays bright colours made the books look exciting. I saw one boys mother buy him four books! Im sure the shop will be a success.

Some English words come from other languages.

 Write the meanings. Use a dictionary if you need help.

chef ______________________________

chauffeur ______________________________

What language are these words originally from? ______________

Spelling Rules! Student Book 4 (ISBN 9780655092704) © Janelle Ho, Helen Pearson

An American boy once boarded a train alone and travelled 160 kilometres – in his sleep!

Say Listen Look Understand Remember Practise	
travel	______
relax	______
journey	______
caravan	______
luggage	______
budget	______
museum	______
attraction	______
entertainment	______
accommodation	______
sightseeing	______
restaurant	______

1 Break each word up into its base word and suffix.

	base word	suffix
attraction		
entertainment		
accommodation		

2 These words can all be used in different ways. Tick boxes to show which ways they can be used.

	noun	verb	adjective
travel	☐	☐	☐
relaxing	☐	☐	☐
journey	☐	☐	☐
budget	☐	☐	☐
sightseeing	☐	☐	☐

3 Complete the table.

word	add s or es	add ed	add ing
relax	______	______	relaxing
journey	journeys	______	______
budget	______	budgeted	______
travel	travels	______	______

Which words above are spelt differently in American English?

______ ______

Spelling Rules! Student Book 4 (ISBN 9780655092704) © Janelle Ho, Helen Pearson

4 Write a word that matches the definition.

____________________ suitcases and other bags

____________________ a place where things from the past are displayed

____________________ a place to eat

____________________ take a trip to another place

____________________ includes hotels, motels and caravans

____________________ what tourists do

____________________ a plan to spend money wisely

Tip

A **mnemonic** is a memory trick.
Caravan starts with ***car*** *and is followed by* ***a van****.*

5 Write or draw your own mnemonic for these words.

restaurant	luggage	accommodation

6 The city or country in which each attraction is found is hidden in each sentence. Circle the letters and write the city/country in the box.

Mr Chupar is afraid of heights and will not be climbing the Eiffel Tower.

Raja panicked when he thought he had to walk up Mount Fuji!

I could not understand our guide at the Taj Mahal because he spoke in dialect.

Sue wrote a poem about the Leaning Tower of Pisa. Her dad thought it a lyrical miracle.

Reflection

- I can do this.
- I am not sure.
- I need help.

Spelling Rules! Student Book 4 (ISBN 9780655092704) © Janelle Ho, Helen Pearson

Unit 35 Revision

The weather on the planet Neptune is seriously extreme. The wind can blow at up to 2000 km/h!

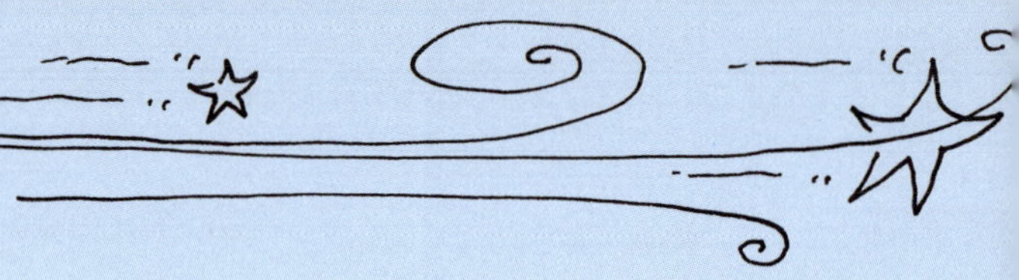

1 Write double consonants to complete these words.

te _ _ ific   su _ _ est   a _ _ raction   ha _ _ ine _ _

pre _ _ ure   so _ _ ow   exce _ _ ent   emba _ _ a _ _

reco _ _ end   sa _ _ hire   a _ _ istant   exa _ _ erate

2 Form antonyms by adding a prefix from the box to each word. Use a different prefix each time.

mis   in   il   un   dis

_____advantage   _____complete   _____pleasant   _____behave   _____logical

3 Write an antonym for each word. (Clue: Each antonym has five letters.)

late ____________   exit ____________   dead ____________

last ____________   end ____________   tight ____________

light ____________   approximate ____________   small ____________

4 Write a synonym for each word. (Clue: Each synonym has an **er** sound, although the spelling might be different.)

happen ____________   diary ____________   outing ____________

fantastic ____________   sure ____________   manners ____________

5 Complete the tables.

verb	noun
	survival
grow	
measure	
	fantasy
	breath

noun	adjective
	logical
guilt	
	courageous
	energetic

Spelling Rules! Student Book 4 (ISBN 9780655092704) © Janelle Ho, Helen Pearson

6 Write a more interesting word for the underlined word or words.

Kerry <u>looked</u> everywhere for the earring she lost. ____________

I was <u>happy</u> that we won the match. ____________

Fawaz was surprised when a kangaroo suddenly <u>came out</u>. ____________

Sam was <u>very tired</u> after the cross-country carnival. ____________

7 These words are sometimes confused. Colour the correct word.

The dog escaped because the [not | knot] had come [lose | loose].

I [wander | wonder] [were | where] I can hide Mum's present.

[Weather | Whether] it rains or not, I [expect | except] we will enjoy our class picnic.

Mum is [vain | vein] and covers the [vain | vein] on her face with make-up.

8 You are spending your holidays in Antarctica. Write a postcard to your friend.

To

____

____

____

____

9 There are too many double letters in this passage. Circle the words that are wrong and write them correctly.

Maiko loves creating art on her computer. She ussually ____________

spends an hour each night emailling her ideas to her ____________

friends. This year she has designed a speciall card and ____________

a personnal present to give to each of her teachers. ____________

On the front is a painting of the sandy dessert with the ____________

teacher wearing a silly hat!

Unit 1
oppose
endure
revise
complete
arrange
escape
persuade
realise
collide
assume
include
declare

Unit 2
copy
hurry
guilty
mystery
variety
deny
apply
simplify
qualify
display
prey
annoy

Unit 3
begin
forget
regret
occur
prefer
enter
offer
answer
visit
happen
target
label
detail

Unit 4
engulf
behalf
cough
trough
phase
phobia
phantom
metaphor
emphasise
biography
amphibian
sophisticated

Unit 5
odd
stiff
err
recall
install
swell
thrill
floss
discuss
possess
witness
embarrass

Unit 7
least
eager
release
dread
ahead
heavy
health
meant
instead
pleasant
jealous
weather

Unit 8
bandage
sponge
surge
stranger
siege
badger
pledge
reject
injection
adjust
conjunction
adjective

Unit 9
bandage
sponge
surge
stranger
siege
badger
pledge
reject
injection
adjust
conjunction
adjective

Unit 10
unfamiliar
undeveloped
unbroken
unquestioning
inactive
incomplete
informal
invisible
disease
disqualify
discontented
discontinue

Unit 11
lose
loose
breath
breathe
desert
dessert
practise
practice
wonder
wander
stationery
stationary

Unit 13
narrow
sorrow
tomorrow
loan
poach
coward
foul
announce
voucher
boundary
council
knowledge

Unit 14
verse
superb
alert
convert
deserve
determined
certain
permanent
earthquake
research
earnest
rehearsal

Unit 15
worthy
senior
surprise
further
burden
survive
journal
flavour
labour
courtesy
honour
nourish

Unit 16
nature
future
capture
failure
creature
feature
measure
pleasure
leisure
adventure
furniture
temperature

Unit 17
ruby
scarlet
lilac
violet
emerald
indigo
crimson
azure
khaki
ochre
turquoise
sapphire

Unit 19
fourth
fifth
eighth
ninth
twelfth
growth
warmth
length
strength
width
depth
breadth

Unit 20
panic
picnic
magic
logic
critic
basic
mimic
fantastic
terrific

energet**ic**
automat**ic**
enthusiast**ic**

Unit 21
capit**al**
hospit**al**
fin**al**
logic**al**
magic**al**
nation**al**
natur**al**
digit**al**
crimin**al**
critic**al**
surviv**al**
emotion**al**

Unit 22
eleven
twelve
thirteen
fourteen
fifteen
twenty
thirty
forty
fifty
ninety
hundred
thousand

Unit 23
a**cc**ept
a**cc**use
a**tt**empt
a**tt**itude
po**ll**ute
a**pp**roach
disa**pp**oint
o**pp**ortunity
nece**ss**ary
reco**mm**end
o**cc**asion
a**gg**re**ss**ive

Unit 25
gin**ge**r
gently
general
avera**ge**
generous
reli**gi**on
intelli**ge**nt
fra**gi**le
generation
advanta**ge**
emer**ge**ncy
gymnasium

Unit 26
seri**ous**
preci**ous**
delici**ous**
fam**ous**
nerv**ous**
danger**ous**
courage**ous**
furi**ous**
cauti**ous**
envi**ous**
spaci**ous**
vari**ous**

Unit 27
less**en**
stiff**en**
tough**en**
sadd**en**
awak**en**
straight**en**
final**ise**
memor**ise**
fantas**ise**
energ**ise**
sympath**ise**
visual**ise**

Unit 28
move**ment**
state**ment**
argu**ment**
amaze**ment**
measure**ment**
govern**ment**
environ**ment**
treat**ment**
develop**ment**
attach**ment**
encourage**ment**
disappoint**ment**

Unit 29
computer
laptop
email
internet
mobile
keyboard
program
icon
download
insert
delete
barcode

Unit 31
n**ie**ce
bel**ie**f
ach**ie**ve
al**ie**n
rec**ei**pt
dec**ei**ve
prot**ei**n
w**ei**rd
r**ei**gn
s**ei**ze
b**ei**ge
f**ei**sty

Unit 32
exist
exchange
examination
explosion
expensive
exaggerate
excursion
exceed
except
extinct
exhausted
exhibition

Unit 33
auth**or**
groc**er**
carpent**er**
lawy**er**
assist**ant**
account**ant**
electric**ian**
politic**ian**
journal**ist**
pharmac**ist**
chef
pilot

Unit 34
travel
relax
journey
caravan
luggage
budget
museum
attraction
entertainment
accommodation
sightseeing
restaurant

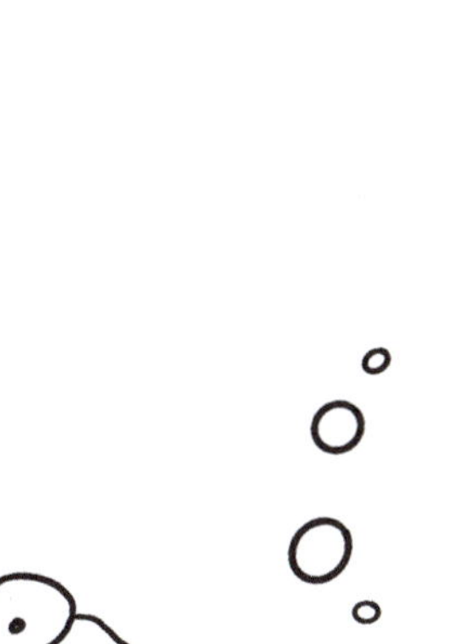

LIST WORDS IN ALPHABETICAL ORDER

accept	Unit 23
accommodation	Unit 34
accountant	Unit 33
accuse	Unit 23
achieve	Unit 31
adjective	Unit 9
adjust	Unit 9
advantage	Unit 25
adventure	Unit 16
aggressive	Unit 23
ahead	Unit 7
alert	Unit 14
alien	Unit 31
amazement	Unit 28
amphibian	Unit 4
announce	Unit 13
annoy	Unit 2
apply	Unit 2
approach	Unit 23
argument	Unit 28
arrange	Unit 1
assistant	Unit 33
assume	Unit 1
attachment	Unit 28
attempt	Unit 23
attitude	Unit 23
attraction	Unit 34
author	Unit 33
automatic	Unit 20
average	Unit 26
awaken	Unit 27
azure	Unit 17
badger	Unit 9
bandage	Unit 9
barcode	Unit 29
basic	Unit 20
begin	Unit 3
behalf	Unit 4
beige	Unit 31
belief	Unit 31
biography	Unit 4
boundary	Unit 13
breadth	Unit 19
breath	Unit 11
breathe	Unit 11
budget	Unit 34
burden	Unit 15
capital	Unit 21
capture	Unit 16
caravan	Unit 34
carpenter	Unit 33
cautious	Unit 26
certain	Unit 14
chef	Unit 33
cleanliness	Unit 8
collide	Unit 1
complete	Unit 1
computer	Unit 29
conclusion	Unit 8
confusion	Unit 8
conjunction	Unit 9
convert	Unit 14
copy	Unit 2
cough	Unit 4
council	Unit 13
courageous	Unit 26
courtesy	Unit 15
coward	Unit 13
creature	Unit 16
criminal	Unit 21
crimson	Unit 17
critic	Unit 20
critical	Unit 21
dangerous	Unit 26
deceive	Unit 31
decision	Unit 8
declare	Unit 1
delete	Unit 29
delicious	Unit 26
deny	Unit 2
depth	Unit 19
desert	Unit 11
deserve	Unit 14
dessert	Unit 11
detail	Unit 3
determined	Unit 14
development	Unit 28
digital	Unit 21
direction	Unit 8
disappoint	Unit 23
disappointment	Unit 28
discontented	Unit 10
discontinue	Unit 10
discuss	Unit 5
disease	Unit 10
display	Unit 2
disqualify	Unit 10
download	Unit 29
dread	Unit 7
eager	Unit 7
earnest	Unit 14
earthquake	Unit 14
eighth	Unit 19
electrician	Unit 33
eleven	Unit 22
email	Unit 29
embarrass	Unit 5
emerald	Unit 17
emergency	Unit 25
emotional	Unit 21
emphasise	Unit 4
encouragement	Unit 28
endure	Unit 1
energetic	Unit 20
energise	Unit 27
engulf	Unit 4
enter	Unit 3
entertainment	Unit 34
enthusiastic	Unit 20
envious	Unit 26
environment	Unit 28
err	Unit 5
escape	Unit 1
exaggerate	Unit 32
examination	Unit 32
exceed	Unit 32
except	Unit 32
exchange	Unit 32
excursion	Unit 32
exhausted	Unit 32
exhibition	Unit 32
exist	Unit 32
expensive	Unit 32
explosion	Unit 32
extinct	Unit 32
failure	Unit 16
famous	Unit 26
fantasise	Unit 27
fantastic	Unit 20
feature	Unit 16
feisty	Unit 31
fifteen	Unit 22
fifth	Unit 19
fifty	Unit 22
final	Unit 21
finalise	Unit 27
flavour	Unit 15
floss	Unit 5
forget	Unit 3
forgetfulness	Unit 8
fourteen	Unit 22
forty	Unit 22
foul	Unit 13
fourth	Unit 19
fragile	Unit 25
furious	Unit 26
furniture	Unit 16
further	Unit 15
future	Unit 16
general	Unit 25
generation	Unit 25
generous	Unit 25
gently	Unit 25
ginger	Unit 25
government	Unit 28
greatness	Unit 8
grocer	Unit 33
growth	Unit 19
guilty	Unit 2
gymnasium	Unit 25
happen	Unit 3
health	Unit 7
heavy	Unit 7
honour	Unit 15
hospital	Unit 21
hundred	Unit 22
hurry	Unit 2
icon	Unit 29
inactive	Unit 10
include	Unit 1

Spelling Rules! Student Book 4 (ISBN 9780655092704) © Janelle Ho, Helen Pearson

SPELLING RULES AND TIPS

Adding es, ed and ing

If a word ends in silent **e**, drop the **e** before adding the suffixes **ed** or **ing**.

smile → smiled *ride → riding*

If a word ends in **y**, change **y** to **i** before adding **es** or **ed**.

try → tries *spy → spied*

But keep the **y** when adding **ing**.

try → trying

If a verb ends in **ic**, when you add **ed** or **ing** add a **k** to keep the hard **c** sound.

mimic → mimicked, mimicking

But the verb stays the same when **s** is added.

mimic → mimics

Adding y

If a word has a single vowel followed by a single consonant, double the consonant before adding **y**.

mud → muddy

If a word ends in silent **e**, drop the **e** before adding **y**.

juice → juicy

Adding ous

If the base word ends in silent **e**, drop the **e** before adding **ous**.

fame → famous

If the base word ends in **ce**, change the **e** to **i** before adding **ous**.

space → spacious

If the base word ends in **ge**, keep the **e** when adding **ous**.

courage → courageous

If the base word ends in **y**, change **y** to **i** before adding **ous**.

envy → envious

Adding ion

Some verbs can be changed into nouns by adding **ion**.

act → action

If the verb ends in silent **e**, drop the **e** before adding **ion**.

create → creation

If the verb ends in **de**, change **de** to **s** before adding **ion**.

divide → division